# The Philosopher

# The Philosopher
## Habermas and Us

PHILIPP FELSCH

Translated by Tony Crawford

polity

Originally published in German by Propyläen Verlag as *Der Philosoph. Habermas und wir* © Philipp Felsch 2024. Published by arrangement with Gaeb & Eggers Literary Agency.

This English translation © Polity Press, 2025.

The translation of this work was supported by a grant from the Goethe-Institut.

Polity Press
65 Bridge Street
Cambridge CB2 1UR, UK

Polity Press
111 River Street
Hoboken, NJ 07030, USA

ISBN-13: 978-1-5095-6769-0 – hardback

Library of Congress Control Number: 2025936422

A catalogue record for this book is available from the British Library.

Typeset in 11 on 14pt Warnock Pro
by Cheshire Typesetting Ltd, Cuddington, Cheshire
Printed and bound in Great Britain by CPI Group (UK) Ltd, Croydon

For further information on Polity, visit our website:
politybooks.com

# Contents

# An Afternoon in Starnberg

It looks as though my forty-minute train ride from Munich's main station has brought me to Long Island: the modernistic bungalow overlooking a wooded slope would be more at home in the Hamptons than in upper Bavaria. The owner of the house looks American to me too, coming to the door in his chinos and brand-new Reeboks.

In spite of his age, Jürgen Habermas makes a slim, sprightly impression. I can't deny feeling a certain awe in his presence. This man in trainers worked closely with Adorno, conversed with Hannah Arendt in New York and Michel Foucault in Paris – and is himself the author of a monumental philosophical *œuvre*. And not only that: even now, seventy years after he entered the German public sphere in the early 1950s, his influence still seems to be tangible in every debate. His political positions with regard to Germany's history continue to influence German commemorative culture. Whether he weighs in on digital media, the Ukraine war or the crisis in the Middle East, he can be sure of national – even international – attention. At over ninety! If they had lived as long, Foucault would have interpreted the election of Donald Trump, Hannah Arendt would have analysed 9/11 and Adorno would have commented on Oliver Bierhoff's golden goal in the 1996 European Championship. In spite of his status as an old white man, Habermas still seems to be indispensable. It is as if what Chancellor Olaf Scholz has named our *Zeitenwende* – the disturbing break with long-cherished beliefs – calls more than anything for a re-examination of his work.

Habermas has been around for as long as I can remember – but as someone I acknowledged more or less out of duty, and whose ideas I received mostly second-hand, and preferably from the point of view of his opponents. Today, that strikes me as negligent. Hadn't he been an indispensable point of reference in my own intellectual development? Hadn't he influenced, as no other, the political discourse of West Germany? What does the passing of the world of yesteryear mean for his legacy? Will Germany be a different country without him?

Although people told me he hardly ever received visitors any more, he immediately answered my written request to talk to him with an invitation to come to Starnberg. Because he no longer travelled, he wrote, he was leaving the date and time up to me. On this Friday afternoon in early June 2022 in Bavaria, the heat feels more like August. A joint search for a vase for the flowers I bought at the train station helps me over my initial timidity. While making tea, Habermas apologizes for the fact that the chocolate marble cake he bought for our meeting is cut too thick.

His unusual-sounding name has been a familiar one to me since my childhood. The Habermas family lived diagonally across from my grandparents in Gummersbach, in a neighbourhood of single-family homes with generous gardens just outside the zone of the 1950s housing estates. Their name was part of the vocabulary of our visits to Gummersbach – just like that of the Bergmanns, whom my grandparents visited to watch television before they could afford their own set; like Adamek's, the grocery shop around the corner, and like *Magerquark*, the low-fat cheese curd that my digestively impaired grandfather spread on his bread. The Habermases too were part of my grandparents' loose-knit neighbourhood network. I remember that my grandmother used to have coffee once in a while with old Mrs Habermas, whose husband had died in the early 1970s, and on one of those occasions – a birthday party, I believe – she also met Mrs Habermas's famous son.

Habermas's reaction to my memories of Gummersbach is reserved – he almost seems embarrassed. He left the town right after finishing school, he says. And because his parents hadn't moved to that house until the 1950s, he only knew it from his sporadic visits. The rather distant relationship to his family of origin seems to be a characteristic of West Germany's postwar generations in general. By this time, he has led me into the living room, where we take seats in the corner with the sofa whose light wool tones have long since entered the iconography of West German intellectual history as the 'communicative epicentre' of the Habermas home. On this sofa, beneath the abstract colour fields of a Günter Fruhtrunk painting titled 'Wiesengrund Daydream' after Theodor Wiesengrund Adorno, which a clueless critic in the 1970s thought must be a landscape, the philosopher of the relations of communication has been photographed at least as often as in front of the obligatory wall-to-wall book-shelves. This is where he has had discussions with many great minds, artists and prominent politicians, including Herbert Marcuse, Wolf Biermann and half the leadership of the Social Democratic Party – a circumstance that heightens my sensation of how unpretentious the atmosphere is. I try to imagine the ceremony that a visit to Jacques Derrida or Peter Sloterdijk might have involved. In the Habermas house, in any case, everything exudes a cultivated normalcy. His wife Ute joins us after a while. With tea and marble cake, with her husband's barely perceptible accent of the area east of Cologne in my ears, I experience my second epiphany of this afternoon: on my arrival, Habermas had looked to me like an American; now

I have a momentary *déjà vu* of those visits to my grandparents in Gummersbach.[1]

Of course, my grandparents' living room would have been dominated by genre paintings in oil and by the dark brown tones and rounded corners of 1950s middle-class nostalgia. Here, on the contrary, is the bright sobriety of postwar modernism – although its austerity is checked by the comfortable sofa group and an antique here and there. The avant-garde of 1960s Critical Theory had at least found living in the new buildings of the ribbon developments, exposed to the brutal inhospitality of the rebuilt cities, conducive to the cultivation of true class consciousness. The fact that Habermas fulfilled his dream of homeownership here, in this idyllic environment, was seen by his contemporaries in the early 1970s as a symbolic act announcing the end of an era. 'Style is lived behaviour', he wrote with regard to Heidegger, who had allowed a photographer to shoot an exclusive photo essay in his Black Forest cabin in 1966. Ten years later, Habermas allowed Barbara Klemm to take portrait photos of him in his house. Was homeowners' philosophy coming into its own? From the 1970s, Habermas's letters were sent from house to house – to Martin Walser, Niklas Luhmann, friends and colleagues sitting in their single-family homes in other corners of West Germany. Was this the only appropriate form of housing for the poets and philosophers of a country whose new urban fringe developments had resolved the historic conflict between the metropolis and the provinces?[2]

While I hasten to steer the conversation away from Gummersbach and my grandparents, and towards the questions that actually brought me here, the scene is disturbed by the muffled rumble of a lawnmower. Those who grew up in the time before leaf blowers came along inevitably associate this noise with the atmosphere of lazy, uneventful summer afternoons. Like the aroma of the famous madeleine that Proust dipped in his tea, it makes my observations of the past hour suddenly crystallize into a whole gestalt. In the 1990s, after German reunification, when many of his colleagues were indulging in fantasies of Germany's new prestige in the world, Habermas had insisted that he wished to remain the citizen of a 'universal-provincial country'.[3] Here, in his sober, comfortable living room, this phrase suddenly becomes intuitively obvious: the mixture of worldliness and provincialism – the Hamptons and Gummersbach; the constellation of lawnmower, mid-century and marble cake – reveals its secret significance: it is symbolic of the old West Germany.

I never would have dreamed that I would one day be sitting with Habermas in his living room. In the 1990s during my studies, when his name crossed my path for the second time, the lines were clearly drawn: Habermas had called my favourite authors of the time, the French philosophers, 'young conservatives', classing them with people like Helmut Kohl and Arnold Gehlen – an offence that some of the French had repaid with outrage and others with indifference. At a chilly dinner in the spring of 1983, when Habermas was teaching at the Collège de France in Paris, Michel Foucault is said to have asked, with his characteristic shark's smile, whether Habermas considered him an anarchist. According to the historian and Foucault translator Ulrich Raulff, he probably would have taken an affirmative answer 'as a compliment'. For my part, I considered Habermas hopelessly fixated, to my existentialist political mind, on the structure of our institutions and their legitimacy. Gilles Deleuze's cutting reference to the 'bureaucrats of pure reason', the ivy-covered administrators of philosophy, seemed to be tailored to him. The Byzantine architecture of his theory was supposed to reunite the True and the Good (if not necessarily the Beautiful), as Hegel's once had done. But when it came to academic styles, I preferred that of his domestic rival Luhmann, who stood for a leaner, meaner way of thinking – with no mercy towards 'neat, helpful' theories born of 'an interest in recognizing and curing'. In comparison with Luhmann's inscrutable laconicism, the streak of self-deprecation that Habermas permitted himself from time to time looked simply antiquated. 'Luhmann wins in the end', as the Luhmann follower Norbert Bolz put it after the turn of the millennium.[4]

I imagined Habermas as being more repelling, ponderous, mandarin. In the course of our conversation, he leans so far back in his sofa, his legs crossed, that his left trainer hovers almost at eye level. Neither his books nor his public appearances had prepared me for the charisma that he displayed in our discussion. As I now know, others before me have had the same experience: there are numerous anecdotes in which Habermas, the putative bureaucrat of pure reason, turns out to be an interested, generous, witty person to talk to. In the early 1960s, as his career was picking up speed, his unadorned, almost casual manner must have had an irresistibly modern air. The Jewish Studies professor Jacob Taubes, who was an adviser together with Habermas to the Suhrkamp publisher Siegfried Unseld, considered him the 'brightest mind of this generation'. His friend the cultural critic Karl Heinz Bohrer said he embodied something 'uniquely new': that is, 'the intellectual invasion of the university'. In those days, the old-school dons still set the tone in the ivy-covered halls, but Habermas was 'at once witty and serious, lively and strict. And he had enormous style in his somewhat frustratingly difficult diction.' The reporters from the left alternative daily *die tageszeitung* (*taz* for short) who visited him in Starnberg in 1980 – and admitted to some 'jitters in the presence of authority' – found him 'lean, agile, very friendly'. Four decades later, I can confirm their impression.[5]

The delegation from the *taz* had some reservations about his middle-class habitus. In any case, the tone taken towards Habermas changed during the 1980s: while he became more acceptable to non-leftist circles, and in 1986 began meeting in an informal working group with the Hessian minister of the environment Joschka Fischer, the reservations that I and my cohort continued to harbour into the 1990s prevailed in the intellectual milieu and among students. Habermas was now accused of having betrayed the legacy of Critical Theory and, in the same breath, of being an unoriginal thinker who cobbled together second-hand ideas – and that in a mindless 'prof jargon', according to Karl Markus Michel, the former Suhrkamp editor and co-editor of the *Kursbuch*. Habermas, who had taken up the opposition to the philosophical style of the mandarins in the 1960s, was suddenly pigeonholed as a scholastic philosopher himself – an image shift that he seems to have registered with regret and borne with equanimity. Playing the role of 'the guardian of rationality' was increasingly vexing, he sighed in 1983.[6]

A violent fantasy by the British author Rachel Cusk is a late echo of the distaste for Habermas: in her 2014 novel *Outline*, a minor character tells about a complex relationship with a male philosophy professor. The man is a Habermas expert. The books and papers he leaves lying around in their flat drive her to desperation, but she literally lacks the strength to fight his mess: 'the works of Jürgen Habermas . . . are as heavy as the stones they used to build the pyramids'. The tables are not turned until she comes home one evening to find that her cats have taken the initiative: 'My novels . . . were untouched: only Habermas had been attacked, his photograph torn from every frontispiece, great claw-marks scorched across *The Structural Transformation of the Public Sphere*.' Her partner puts his things away from then on to prevent further damage.[7]

I am struck not only by the deep satisfaction that the narrator seems to feel, above and beyond her relationship issues, at the destruction of Habermas's books, but also by the philosopher's dubious fame expressed in her aversion to him. On the other hand, what contemporary thinker should Cusk have chosen as an icon of scholasticism? The French have the reputation – whether deserved or not – of being rebels against academic convention. And the Americans are too unknown outside university walls. As early as the 1970s, the publisher of French philosophy Axel Matthes certified that Habermas was a 'brand name'. Not only the man, wrote Ronald Dworkin, but 'his fame itself is famous'. Perhaps 'Habermas' had long since ceased to refer to an individual philosopher, had become a label with global recognition as representing a certain style of thinking.[8]

Over the course of the afternoon, as the June sun wanders across the bay windows of the Habermas house, we talk about Adorno and Foucault, New York and Jerusalem; about what the Suhrkamp culture and German unification meant to him. Only at the very end do we get round to talking about the war that broke out four months ago in Ukraine. Habermas's initial statement on the war, just recently published in the *Süddeutsche Zeitung*, has brought him a great deal of criticism for advocating the German chancellor's cautious stance. Without disguising his consternation, the man who has always been able to rely on his sense of the zeitgeist explains that, 'for the first time', he feels he no longer understands the reactions of the German public.

It has grown late. A short time afterwards, we say good-bye. On the way back to Munich, I have an almost poignant feeling of having experienced the end of something. But what? The end of a seventy-year-long relationship between an intellectual and his audience? The end of the old West Germany, of which I had a vision that afternoon in Habermas's living room?[9]

In spite of mild doubts about my project of writing a book about him, he granted me access to his archived papers. In the year and a half that have passed since then, I have immersed myself in his correspondence in the archive centre of the University of Frankfurt. It is characteristic of Habermas that he has ceded his papers not to the august German Literature Archives in Marbach, but here, where they can be read in the pale fluorescent light of an antiquated ambience. Loyalty to his old institution seems to be more important to him than accession to the German pantheon.

Reading and rereading Habermas's published writings proved to be a double-edged exercise: his principal works are still as discouragingly hermetic as I remembered them. On the other hand, I have discovered Habermas the political commentator, critic and polemicist, deploying in the debating forum a stylistic brilliance that he seems to eschew deliberately in his academic texts. The various puzzle pieces formed a picture of a thinker both rigorous and contradictory. As a philosopher, he strove as few others for the timeless and universal, while as a public intellectual he responded – in practically all his interventions – to the specific historical situation that had resulted from the aftermath of Nazism in Germany. Although he has, with extraordinary insistence, kept the two roles separate since the 1980s, their interleaving – the alternation between distance and engagement, the dialectics of universalism and particularism – is what characterizes his *œuvre*. Habermas is therefore a more or less ideal figure through whom we can survey the peculiar interrelation of theory, history and memory that is so characteristic of the intellectual terrain of West Germany. Several generations of readers have examined themselves in the mirror of his works over the course of his endless career. Their response to him says at least as much about them as about the philosopher: in addition to everything else, Habermas is a kind of historical–philosophical litmus test. For my part, as I delved into his biography and his work, I felt I saw the intellectual silhouette of my own generation more distinctly in contrast.[10]

# In the Upside-Down World

Those who ask why Habermas seems to embody the old West Germany, and at least a part of the reunited Germany, inevitably have to talk about *his* generation. The space that his generation takes up, not only in postwar Germany's political and cultural makeup, but also in its self-image, is indicated by the many labels that have been tacked onto that cohort: the flak auxiliaries, the sceptics, the twenty-niners, the forty-fivers and, most recently, the fifty-eighters. The 1929 vintage in particular has brought forth so many great names that it is hard to keep them all in mind: Hans Magnus Enzensberger and Dorothee Sölle, Christa Wolf and Heiner Müller, Harald Juhnke and Eduard Zimmermann, Ralf Dahrendorf – and of course Jürgen Habermas. It may be tempting to attribute it to the influence of favourable stars, if it weren't for the historic reasons – the journalist Günter Gaus, also born in 1929, once called it the 'mercy of a later birth' – that help to explain the success of that vintage. The forty-fivers – the label that fits Habermas best – found themselves ideally prepared for a new beginning: too young to be seriously compromised, but old enough to realize that an era had ended. Habermas is the last person who would deny having had this head

start. After the turn of the millennium, he wrote to Martin
Walser, two years his senior, that he saw himself 'and all
of us, yourself included, *always* as the undeserving benefi-
ciaries of a historical constellation that fell to us in postwar
Germany'.[1]

The forty-fivers have been lauded for their political virtues –
their realism, optimism and inventiveness. According to the
writer Florian Illies, the 'intellectual life skills' of the 1929
cohort are defined by the 'belief in the possibility of a second
and better life' – a belief that they share, not with Illies and
my generation, but with those of our age group on the other
side of the Iron Curtain. On one of the stacks of books in
Habermas's living room, I saw the memoirs of the Albanian
political scientist Lea Ypi, in which she recapitulates her life
before and after the end of actually existing socialism. 'When
you see a system change once, it's not that difficult to believe
that it can change again', she writes about the lesson of those
years – a sentiment that must have been immediately obvious
to her reader in Starnberg.[2]

Habermas too, who has described on various occasions
how the radio reports on the Nuremberg trials and the Allies'
documentation of Bergen-Belsen opened his eyes to the true
nature of Nazism, believed a political reset was possible. 'We
believed that a spiritual and moral renewal was indispensable
and inevitable', he recalled thirty years later. Great hopes were
attached to that renewal. He had felt the need for a 'spontaneous sweeping away, some explosive act, which then could have
served to begin the formation of a political entity'.[3] In that sentiment he expresses a longing for purification, for revolution
and redemption, which has something zealous, millenarian,
about it, rather than the reformist temperament that he was
later reputed to have.

Right at the founding of West Germany, in the winter term
of 1949, the twenty-year-old Habermas enrolled in the university of my home town, Göttingen. A series of disappointments

began immediately with the formation of the first Bonn government, which included two national-conservative ministers; it continued with West Germany's rearmament, its anti-Communist stance and the failure of denazification. The 'politics of normalization of an old man with a limited vocabulary', as Habermas called the first chancellor, belied hopes for a fresh start. Ralf Dahrendorf called Habermas a true 'grandchild of Adenauer', but although he later advocated integration with an ideal West, the young Habermas supported the idea of a demilitarized, neutral Germany and in 1953 voted for the 'All-German People's Party' of the renegade CDU member Gustav Heinemann. Habermas's attitude towards the 'Bonn Republic' was shaped by the belief that a historic opportunity had been missed – and his relation to the current 'Berlin Republic', which in his view emerged from yet another tainted foundation, is analogous. The gulf between the promise and the reality, between the possible and the actual, became the driving force behind his critical social theory.[4]

One of the paradoxes of his educational career is that Habermas, who had begun reading extensive philosophical works while still in secondary school, enunciated his opposition to the new normalcy with reference to Martin Heidegger – who, as we know since the publication of his 'Black Notebooks', was in those years a paragon of maudlin self-righteousness. The book and theatre reviews and the topical essays that Habermas wrote from the early 1950s on for the *Frankfurter Allgemeine Zeitung* and other newspapers have an unmistakable Heidegger vibe. In defining philosophy's task as 'by aesthesis to unlock the destiny of Being', in advocating against an 'existence of self-assertion, of making available, of planning imposition', and in saying 'that we have lost the proper relationship to "things"', Habermas was translating his discontent with the times into the dualism of authentic and inauthentic life that seems to have been almost unavoidable to critics of culture of every political persuasion in those days. Habermas called on the older professors 'who still define the profile of the universities' to catch up on their reading and finally engage in 'an objective discussion' with Heidegger, while preparing his contemporaries generally for an 'act of inversion': 'Man must take on an attitude of listening to the things and learning to let them be, instead of dominating them.'[5]

The idea of 'inversion' and the dualism of 'utility' and 'awareness' are also key concepts in his 1954 dissertation on Friedrich Wilhelm Joseph Schelling's 'Ages of the World' fragments. In these unfinished writings, Schelling broke with the subjective philosophy of German Idealism and turned instead to a mystical tradition, going back through Pietism to the esoteric teachings of the Jewish Kabbala and the Gnosticism of late antiquity, which interpreted the world as a system of decay waiting for the spark of inversion, since the divine hierarchy of love and hate, light and darkness, good and evil has been perverted into its negation.[6]

Is there also in the philosophy of the all-too-earnest, all-too-rational Habermas a Gnostic idea of decay and a burning core of mystical longing for redemption that can be traced back to his earliest intellectual influences? In what may be the most candid interview he ever gave, he said that something is 'deeply amiss' in our society. His philosophy, on the other hand, is based on a fundamental intuition that draws on religious sources: that is, a notion of 'felicitous' forms of human coexistence 'in which autonomy and dependency can truly enter into a non-antagonistic relation'. In the paired concepts of ideology and self-reflexion, instrumental and communicative reason, system and lifeworld, has Habermas exhaustively explored the dualism of a perverted world and the hope for redemption that he alludes to here? Can that dualism also be found in his notion of a different, 'post-national' Germany? It makes sense, in view of the convulsions and expectations of the year 1945, that he yielded to the fascination of Heidegger and Schelling, of the mystic Jakob Böhme and the kabbalist Isaac Luria, and that these thinkers gave him the means to immunize himself against the disappointments to come.[7]

Habermas's greatest disappointment was to be the discovery that Heidegger himself refused to re-evaluate his political past. In the 1953 book publication of the introductory lectures on metaphysics that he had originally given in 1935, Heidegger persisted in mentioning the 'inner truth and greatness' of Nazism; that prompted Habermas to call out the philosopher he had once found so authoritative in an article in the *FAZ*. 'Can the planned murder of millions of people, which we all know about today, be explained in terms of Being as a fatal mistake?' That was the question with which Habermas made his debut as a brilliant polemicist on the West German scene. It would be going too far to say he broke with Heidegger: the import of his critique lay in the argument that Heidegger, by stubbornly defending an error that seemed to manifest the pathology of a whole society, was falling short of his own pioneering conception of temporality, which required questioning the past from time to time 'as something . . . yet to come'. Very generally, Habermas defended content against style and the categories Heidegger had developed in *Being and Time* against the vulgarity of their political appropriation. It was time, Habermas concluded with dialectical finesse, 'to think with Heidegger against Heidegger'.[8]

Jacob Taubes later claimed to have seen 'the whole Habermas' in this phrase – a claim that is not without support. By supplanting the isolated subject of the Cartesian tradition with an intrinsically involved Being-in-the-world, Heidegger had pointed the way towards post-metaphysical philosophy. But he had not gone far enough. He had interpreted human existence as a network of involvements, but not of communication. Because communication with others, from the perspective of his heroic nihilism, boiled down to the lamentable state of 'surrender to the They', Heidegger had been unable to perceive the interactive dimension of *Dasein*. It was left to his reader Habermas to correct this omission.[9]

And Heidegger himself? A reader of the *Frankfurter Allgemeine Zeitung* who had not failed to see the attack, he noted incredulously that its author 'Habermaas' (*sic*) was an unknown, twenty-four-year-old student. He did not feel called upon to issue a rebuttal – on the contrary, as he wrote to his wife in August 1953, he had 'purposely not looked at a newspaper' since then.[10]

# Perpetrators and Victims

Another philosopher, one diametrically opposed to Heidegger, also took notice of the student. In 1956 Adorno hired Habermas as an assistant at the Institute for Social Research in Frankfurt. 'I felt like a figure from a novel by Balzac', Habermas recalled; 'the awkward and uneducated boy from the country whose eyes are opened by the city.' The Jewish remigrant's milieu, which included such visitors as Herbert Marcuse and Gershom Scholem, must have been utterly fascinating. In 1956, the kid from the provinces who had just realized that not only Heidegger but also the professors who had supervised his dissertation had been Nazis, arrived not just in the big city, but in the circles of the very man who – according to the social psychologist Christian Schneider – spoke with the voice of the victims in the land of the perpetrators. In one of the rare peeks he permitted into his emotions, Habermas said he had loved Adorno 'in a way'. If we may believe Ralf Dahrendorf, who had come to the Institute two years before as Max Horkheimer's assistant, but then fled again after two months, neither of the directors was exactly nurturing in their treatment of new staff members. The word going around about Habermas was that his speech impediment made him 'only good for research'. He too seems to have thought about fleeing at first. But although Horkheimer soon wanted him gone again because of his political views, Adorno chose him as a partner for intellectual conversation and began confronting him with his newest ideas. While Habermas had the good fortune to experience the 'lava of thought in flow', his elders, for their part, pinned hopes on him. In reminiscences on those years, a remarkable detail stands out: long before Benjamin-mimicry became fashionable among West Berlin's '68 generation, Habermas reminded both Gretel Adorno and Gershom Scholem of the young Walter Benjamin, in whose high forehead Scholem had seen a gift for metaphysics. Theodor Adorno found Habermas early on to be surrounded by 'a kind of nimbus'.[1]

Did Habermas, thirty years their junior and the son of German parents who had complied with the regime, feel a temptation to identify with the other side in the parallel universe of the Frankfurt School? It is conspicuous that his eldest child, born before he was hired at the Institute, was given the Germanic name Tilmann, while his daughters, who are younger, bear the Old Testament names Rebekka and Judith. In a 1961 radio lecture, Habermas examined the long line of Jewish protagonists of German intellectual history – from Moses Mendelssohn to Georg Simmel, from Isaac Luria to Horkheimer and Adorno. As he informed his listeners, he saw that work as an overdue act of self-verification that was necessary for his own intellectual existence. Had he not been given the task, as Adorno's student, of continuing and revitalizing that tradition that the Nazis had tried to destroy physically? I hear an echo of such a sense of predestined alliance in his thoughts on a post-national German identity when he talks about the phenomenon of survivor guilt, first observed in Holocaust survivors. It was in the late 1980s, shortly after the *Historikerstreit* – the debate in the West German press about the significance of the Nazi period and the Holocaust in contemporary history – that Habermas asked himself and his

German readers: 'But, since that moral catastrophe, doesn't the survival of all of us stand under the curse, in attenuated form, of having merely escaped?'[2]

At the same time, Habermas recalled how shocked he was to be taught by Gershom Scholem that an unbridgeable gulf separates the victim and the perpetrator groups, and that it cannot be closed by some premature rapprochement. At the 1966 session of the World Jewish Congress in Brussels, Scholem had stated unequivocally that the German–Jewish symbiosis, however broken, which Habermas had claimed in his radio lecture to be an influence in his own thinking, had always been asymmetrical and hence misguided, and indeed one of the causes of the catastrophe. Habermas remembers the defensive reaction that these words evoked in him: 'Hadn't we just recognized the streams of Jewish productivity in the best traditions – the only ones that outlasted the corruption . . . ? Did we not stand under the dominant intellectual influences of Marx, Freud, and Kafka? Were we not accepted as students by those (such as Bloch, Horkheimer, Adorno, Plessner, and Löwith) who had returned from exile?'[3]

Scholem's criticism of Jewish 'self-abandonment' implied, if not a call for Jews' complete withdrawal from German intellectual life, then at least a stark dissociation. Habermas meanwhile had not only linked his own future to that of German–Jewish philosophy: he felt the hour of such philosophy was beginning only now, after the catastrophe. Of course he reversed the vector of identification – and this may have won him Scholem's sympathy: it was no longer up to the Jews to earn a right to social existence by assimilating; it was the Germans who must earn a right to the Jewish tradition, 'even and precisely after Auschwitz', by adopting the perspective of those who had escaped the disaster. It all depended, he explained, on 'direct[ing] at ourselves a gaze of those exiles who were schooled in Marx, Freud, and Kafka, upon ourselves, in order to identify the estranged, the repressed, the rigidified parts in ourselves as something split off from life'.[4] This idea, which he expounded in his 1977 speech on Scholem's eightieth birthday in Jerusalem, indicates the retroactive legitimation of his own position as speaker.

In his 1961 radio essay, Habermas admitted with some dismay that he had not been aware that 'half of the scholars named' were Jews. According to Scholem, such ignorance must become impossible in the future Germany. If a true German–Jewish dialogue should ever resume – or rather, begin for the first time – then it must be on the condition that Jews would speak as Jews, and Germans would hear and acknowledge them as Jews. In spite of his scepticism, Scholem must have felt hopeful in view of the developments in West Germany. While the history of Jewish assimilation, or the 'non-Jewish Jews', to borrow a term from the Polish–Jewish historian Isaac Deutscher, could be extended by another chapter on East Germany – think of the Jewish communists who returned from emigration to devote themselves to building the new East German state – in West Germany that history came to an end. The Jewish remigrants who spoke up publicly in West Germany did so in the name of the victims. In allusion to Deutscher's figure of the 'non-Jewish Jew', the Australian historian Dirk Moses, whose critique of the 'catechism' of German commemorative policy caused a considerable stir some years ago, described the West German character of the 'non-German German'. In the quest for absolution for the sins of the past, the 'non-German German' strove to adopt a collective identity committed to universalist principles and divorced from tradition and history. Identifying messianic traits in the West German 'redemptive republicanism', Moses saw Habermas as its type specimen.[5]

# Farewell to Profundity

Habermas has written an essay in praise of essay-writing which is one of his most elegant texts: the foreword to a collection of his pieces about Adorno, Hannah Arendt, Ernst Bloch and other German–Jewish intellectuals, published by Reclam in 1978. The 'lesser degree of rigor' that essays display in comparison to systematic philosophical exposition is made up for by their 'topicality', their 'greater effectiveness in shaping public opinion' and the opportunity they offer for a 'more candid advocacy' and 'more agile associations'. Among the scholars to whom he devoted his essays, Habermas also saw a 'high sensitivity to the latently anarchical' and to 'diffuse changes in configurations with great historical implications'. In situations of social and cultural change, more can be learned 'from those who are more versed in the perception of symptoms'.[1]

According to a widely held opinion, Habermas himself is not a member of that perceptive category. Although Adorno was able to persuade him of the topicality of a critique along Marxian lines, Habermas felt Adorno's way of philosophizing was no longer in keeping with the times. Not only did his boss, illuminated by the 'self-evident truths', ignore the expanding universe of secondary literature, but he had basically stopped reading even before the war, Habermas soon realized, and limited himself to working with a handful of classics. To counteract such a snobbism of literary intelligence, Habermas adopted a 'more systematic approach'. It may well be that Adorno was all too glad to leave the grunt work of biblio-graphic research to his assistant. In any case, processing large quantities of literature has been a characteristic of Habermas's style of thinking and writing ever since. Even his habilitation thesis, published as *The Structural Transformation of the Public Sphere* – still his best-selling book today – owed its existence, as the preface to the second edition proclaims, to the 'synthesis of an almost unmanageable wealth of contributions from several disciplines'. And the same is true, perhaps more so, of the 1981 two-volume *Theory of Communicative Action*, in which the author evaluated ten years of interdisciplinary research. And Habermas can certainly be accused of exces-sive modesty for introducing his late work, the 2,000-page *histoire croisée* of philosophy and religion titled *Also a History of Philosophy* (his birthday present to himself and his readers on turning ninety in 2019), with the remark that his age all but prevented him from doing justice to the pertinent 'libraries of secondary literature'.[2]

In describing his writing style, Habermas prefers botanical metaphors: 'When I have found an interesting flower or herb, I try to figure out how it will fit together with others, whether it can create a bouquet or pattern.' According to Axel Honneth, who published a defence of Habermas's art of arrangement in *Merkur* in the 1970s, his way of writing was a necessary consequence of the content of his philosophy. Just as Adorno could only undertake his critique of instrumental reason in the unsystematic form of essays to avoid regressing into the pernicious attitude of seizing the object, so too Habermas's communicative theory of society can only be presented dialog-ically: 'The formal structure of Habermas's theory is oriented towards intersubjective communication, not towards stylistic

resistance against instrumental rationality: its form of presentation and its design principle are constructed in response to
discussions that make science possible. Thus the theory itself is
grounded in the form of discussions.'[3]
    Was Habermas the Socrates of West Germany? Not quite:
the form of dialogue that he practised, which he himself once
described as 'rather brutal' assimilation, has little in common
with the Socratic method. Does not the bibliographic appetite
of his *œuvre* reveal more the mentality of the reconstruction
years – as if the tendency to overexertion among the 'heart-
attack generation' had rubbed off on its intellectuals as well?
A 1964 letter from Hans-Ulrich Wehler, a classmate of his
from Gummersbach and later a professor of social history at
Bielefeld, is symptomatic; in it, Wehler describes how he was
'quite groggy' on returning from a research trip in the USA. He
had worked in archives in New York and Chicago for several
weeks, he wrote, 'from 8 in the morning until 12 at night',
reading sources relevant to his habilitation thesis on American
imperialism – until he couldn't go on any longer. His doctors
had diagnosed 'severe exhaustion'. Wehler had been an ambitious middle-distance runner until sometime in the 1950s, and
only his 'athlete's heart', he wrote, had saved him from worse
harm.[4]
    Habermas described his generation's task more than once as
'abolishing profundity'. Were the forty-fivers transforming the
heroism of tendentious, pathetic philosophy that he had criticized in Heidegger into a heroism of overachievement? In his
journals from the late 1970s, Martin Walser, another member
of this generation with whom Habermas was on friendly terms
at that time, described a meeting at which Habermas came
around to the subject of the 'requirement of academic rigour
in philosophy: there is always another book you have to read,
a relevant one. Apparently the academics strangle each other
by forcing each other to read everything any of them writes.
The one who publishes sooner coerces the other more than the

other coerces him – until the next book.' The ironic, almost sarcastic distance from the standards of university research expressed in these lines may well be Walser's addition. On the other hand, who knows? After all, Habermas's interest in dealing with literary authors certainly seems to suggest some reservations against academia, and maybe he had vented his feelings to Walser.[5]

But what Peter Sloterdijk contemptuously called 'genius of the paraphrase' is more than academic pedantry or athletic ambition. In his critique of Heidegger, Habermas had declared 'genius', the pose of original thinking, to be 'ambiguous'. 'The thinker as life-style, as vision, as expressive self-portrait', he wrote in the 1980s, 'is no longer possible.' His oath of abstinence: he was 'not a producer of a *Weltanschauung*'. With almost merciless resolution, he seems to have spurned the legacy of the aesthetic avant-gardes: no lofty, mystical theses, no suggestive images, no prophecies, long-term or short. In his eyes, such dishonest means were used only by irresponsible minds – a category in which he included, from 1968 on if not before, the poet Hans Magnus Enzensberger, a fellow member of the 1929 cohort. Unlike Enzensberger, Habermas was a 'lamentably earnest' person, he wrote with caustic irony, and furthermore 'very seldom euphoric' – and his cool mood sometimes soberingly infects those who read his books.[6]

The sociologist Heinz Bude, who wrote portraits of West Germany's influential sociologists in the early 1990s, felt 'as if this generation' – that is, the forty-fivers – 'had consciously decided not to produce any intellectual brilliance'. Habermas's motto about thinking against Heidegger can be read in a similar vein. To purge his discipline of 'its rhetorical element' and prevent the mixture of theory and literature, which he condemned in the 1980s as a bad habit of his heideggerous French antagonists, he seems to have purposely adopted an unwieldy nominal style – which led many readers to see him as an authority and an eminent scholar, but by no means a

writer. 'Habermas's own voice?', asked the West Berlin sociology professor Urs Jaeggi in 1981: 'It's hiding behind others. It
explains, expands, expatiates. The authorship becomes unim-
portant.' But couldn't that style have an altogether different
meaning? At bottom, Habermas's work is the only writing in
which the 'death of the author' that Roland Barthes proclaimed
in 1967 really happened. With his impersonal diction and his
paraphrasing, he makes the subject disappear in the rush of
discourse much more rigorously than the stylists from France.[7]

# The Consciousness of the Present

One of the ironies of Habermas's reception is that he was once the man of the hour precisely because he liked to process vast quantities of material, even if later readers interpreted that as a lack of originality. The critique of a 'society which had become completely opaque', as Siegfried Kracauer wrote to the Suhrkamp editor Karl Markus Michel in the mid-1960s, called for more than 'just half-reasoned opinions . . . Maybe the difficult present moment calls for the old intellectuals to be relieved by scholars who are also "intellectuals" – I'm thinking of Habermas, for example.' Conservative observers too, such as Arnold Gehlen, noted that the literary intelligentsia were overwhelmed by the complexity of society. Habermas, who wanted to overcome the 'illuminating exercise' of Adorno's negative dialectics through the fervour of scholarly work, may be seen as the Frankfurt School's answer to this deficiency.[1]

The scholar and the public intellectual – the two roles that Habermas took on in a tension-filled balancing act – seemed in the 1960s to be one and the same. The reason has a great deal to do with the magic word 'theory', that shorthand for new thinking that broke with the educational ideal of the Humboldtian university. While philosophy, once the central luminary of the humanities, expounded the meaning of existence or the same old classics, theory considered itself, in Jacob Taubes's expression with Hegelian overtones, the 'consciousness of the present'. If we look for a face that might have embodied that consciousness, we inevitably come to Habermas. 'Habermas brings a new current to philosophy', Taubes wrote to him in 1964, apparently unafraid of currying favour. But he was right – and the recipient of his compliments in turn had no compunction about certifying, in a variation on Plessner's topos of Germany as a 'delayed nation', that all of German postwar philosophy was hopelessly behind the times. Only Germany, the land of poets and philosophers, conserved 'a peculiar form of the mind, a form that had already crumbled elsewhere'.[2]

Habermas, on the other hand, advocated linking philosophy both with the research agenda of the individual disciplines and with political praxis. His appearances as a young professor can be read as attempts to define the new style of thinking. In his 1961 inaugural lecture as adjunct professor in Marburg, he rejected both the classical, Aristotelian and the modern, Hobbesian versions of political philosophy, advocating instead a 'dialectical theory of society' that 'at every step is guided and permeated by the self-consciousness of its own relationship to praxis'. Four years later, that motif would stand out still more prominently in his inaugural lecture in Frankfurt on 'Knowledge and Human Interests'. Apparently stressed more by his father's presence than by that of his renowned colleagues, Habermas began his lecture with a critique of the ancient conception of *theoria*, which had taken the dispassionate 'contemplation of the cosmos' as an ideal of both knowledge and life – an attitude of stoical serenity that had been disastrously coupled with positivism since the nineteenth century, and renewed in *epoché*, the theoretical disposition upheld by the founder of phenomenology, the Jewish scholar Edmund Husserl, even in the 1930s, after the Nazis had destroyed his academic career.

The theory for which Habermas argued instead rejected that attitude. Heidegger, the conservative revolutionary, had taken a resolute posture, in contrast to the contemplative abstinence of his teacher; after the war, Adorno in his turn had pitted the pathos of consternation against Heidegger's heroic style of philosophy. The style of the young Habermas, for all its cool sobriety, reveals something of both Heidegger's and Adorno's attitudes – attitudes that lent a higher tone to the philosophical discourse of the twentieth century. 'This excitability' is what makes scholars public intellectuals, he explained in reference to the German–Jewish essayists he admired. He may as well have been referring to himself, too.[3]

It seems to have been more or less inevitable that Siegfried Unseld, the Suhrkamp publisher who had already courted him as an author, made him an adviser for his new *Theorie* series in 1963. There was no question, as far as Unseld and his editor Karl Markus Michel were concerned, that the series was custom-made for him. When Habermas tried to retire from that function after just three years because of the incessant quarrels with the other advisers (who included Taubes and the philosopher Dieter Henrich), Michel intervened on the spot. 'I told him very plainly that the series had been conceived with a view to his collaboration', he reported to Unseld, 'and that we would not be interested in publishing it if he withdrew.' Enzensberger too, who launched the journal *Kursbuch* in the mid-1960s, let Habermas know 'that the periodical I have started cannot go on without you, and was designed for you'. It is hard to escape the impression that every West German media enterprise that considered itself in any way progressive, or at least contemporary, vied for his collaboration. Even the tabloid publisher Springer, which would become a target of protesting students not least thanks to Habermas's study *The Structural Transformation of the Public Sphere*, made him an offer.[4]

On the occasion of the sixtieth birthday of the Suhrkamp editor Günther Busch in 1989, shortly before the fall of the Berlin

Wall, Habermas delivered a sentimental paean to the theory paperback. Some books, he said, are irreversibly linked with the historical context in which they appeared: 'You can't remember the text without imagining the title page, without seeing in your mind's eye the colour and format of the cover in which we first encountered the title, without seeing the font in which it was set, without feeling the smell and sound of a yellowed topicality which once gave the title its emblematic quality, in which it once unfurled its acuity.' This was the case with Suhrkamp classics such as Adorno's *Jargon der Eigentlichkeit* [*The Jargon of Authenticity*], Marcuse's *Konterrevolution und Revolte* [*Counterrevolution and Revolt*] and Alexander Mitscherlich's *Die Unwirtlichkeit unserer Städte* ['The inhospitality of our cities']. But Habermas could have mentioned his own books as well – *Knowledge and Human Interests, Technology and Science as 'Ideology'*, or *Legitimation Crisis* – among those of the late 1960s and early '70s that bore their own particular aura. In the late 1950s, Adorno and Enzensberger viewed the paperback as a vehicle of the culture industry, but over the decade that followed it became a medium of subversive messages. And unlike Enzensberger, who in his 1958 radio feature 'An Analysis of Paperback Book Production' was still evoking the horror scenario of culture degenerating into commodities and reading flattening out into consumption, the paperback author Habermas realized in the early 1960s that the book market in this case was exercising 'the emancipatory function of an exclusively economic easing of access'. In other words, the contents of paperbacks remained unaffected 'by the laws of mass production to which they owe their distribution'.[5]

By implication, difficult thinking was particularly suited to dissemination in soft covers. Gunter Hofmann, a future journalist who heard Habermas lecture in the early 1960s in Heidelberg, remembered 'how dark, strange and highly complicated' the young professor's remarks seemed to him. In the climate of postwar modernism, however, with its affinity to abstraction, that difficult diction had a peculiar attraction. Nowadays, as ideas that are not immediately comprehensible quickly set off bullshit alarms, we have become estranged from the notion that the unintelligible and the semi-intelligible, the inaccessible and the hermetic once exuded a fascination all their own. 'True thoughts are those alone', says Adorno's *Minima Moralia*, 'which do not understand themselves.'[6]

The speed with which the new, obscure language of theory spread through West German society in those days is indicated by the change of heart of Hans Paeschke, editor in chief of *Merkur*, who, in 1965, had initially rejected 'Knowledge and Human Interests'. 'I won't make the mistake again', he wrote to Habermas three years later, 'of advancing doubts about the educational and communicative level of the average *Merkur* reader. If that reader hasn't learned by now the concepts with which the students who matter argue, as you do, then he's practically not an intellectually worthwhile fellow.' Even such a successful author as Max Frisch felt the need to pay tribute to theory. After he had worked his way through *Knowledge and Human Interests*, the expanded book version of Habermas's inaugural lecture in Frankfurt, he wrote to the author, to whom he had been introduced by their publisher Unseld, to express his esteem. At his age, Frisch wrote, he was not likely to master 'the language of sociology . . . Thus I follow your thinking rather as one who leans over the fence without being able to enter the arena of discussion, taciturn, fascinated and not always quite catching on, meanwhile thoroughly perplexed in his own language; hence he must have understood some-thing after all.'[7]

One thing that ultimately seems to have contributed to Habermas's aura is his rare ability to free the German social sci-ences from their provincialism and lead them towards the state of current international scholarship. In the new *Theorie* series that they edited for Suhrkamp, Jacob Taubes hoped to 'bring ideas to the German discussion from abroad, and so attain the

level of discussion abroad in twenty years'. The Springer journalist Georg Ramseger, who tried in the mid-1960s to recruit
Habermas as a reviewer for the supplement *Literarische Welt*,
modelled after the *Times Literary Supplement*, received the
reply that the 'new philosophical and sociological books of
German origin' were not very fertile ground. 'For this reason,
if for no other, the scope would also have to include (Western)
literature from abroad as well.'[8]

# The Centre Does Not Hold

My father attended the same Gummersbach grammar school as Habermas, although ten years later. Among his formative educational experiences was a French teacher who smoked in class and who took my father along in the late 1950s on a trip to Paris, from which he came home a Francophile. His eyes still shine today when he gets an opportunity to speak French, and although he later lived in the United States for a while, that country and its language and culture have always been foreign to him.

Habermas seems to have had the opposite experience. Asked which foreign country was most important for him after the war, he answers without a second's hesitation: 'America!' After all, that is where everything new came from. Even though, as a student, he cycled all the way to the Mediterranean coast of France, and later was fond of taking his children to Brittany in the summer holidays, his cognitive interests pointed towards America. France or the USA – that seems to have been an existential choice for young West Germans in those days. While the French philosopher Lucien Goldmann tried in vain to recruit him for a colloquium in Paris, Habermas undertook his first transatlantic Grand Tour in the spring of 1965. The rising young star of the Frankfurt School is not often seen in such a humble pose: he confessed to his host in New York, the media sociologist Rolf Meyersohn, that he felt the 'trepidations of a provincial European coming to the New World for the first time'. The prospect of seeking acceptance among New York intellectuals seems to have terrified him. He travelled on to Boston, Chicago and Santa Barbara, met with the emigrants Bruno Bettelheim and Leo Löwenthal, took part in a teach-in in Ann Arbor, and sat for the first time in front of a television set, the nefarious political effects of which he had investigated in his habilitation thesis. But mainly he seems to have made a good impression in New York's intellectual scene. How great must have been his satisfaction when, after his return, Meyersohn attested to his assimilation: 'I don't know why you ever pretended you weren't a real American!' To judge by his outfit, he would never do so again.[1]

Two years later, in late summer of 1967, when the West German student movement was entering its heated phase after the death of Benno Ohnesorg, Habermas flew to New York again, this time with his family, to teach for a semester at the New School for Social Research. During that visit, he met the sociologist Daniel Bell and the political theorist Hannah Arendt. The latter inducted him into her entourage of male admirers, who also included W. H. Auden and Uwe Johnson. The protagonists of the Suhrkamp culture seem to have been all over New York in the late 1960s: Enzensberger walked up to Habermas in the street; he was just finishing a fellowship at Wesleyan University in Connecticut before travelling on to Havana in January 1968.[2]

The Habermases borrowed the apartment of the Meyersohns, who were in London at the time; the two older children went to the Rudolf Steiner School on the Upper East Side. Students at the New School impressed their visiting professor with their critical, politicized awareness, which he saw as ideologically unbiased in comparison with the German 'hotheads'. The easy-going relations with American Jews must have impressed him in particular. 'We joined in the Rosh Hashanah festivities in the park as if we belonged there', Habermas wrote to the Mitscherlichs in Germany. However, he admitted that there were also 'less reassuring aspects' of American day-to-day life. In his letter he describes a Manhattan that was simply overwhelming: 'To start with, my full interest is in understanding the political scene below the level of the parties: Black power, the New Left, the hippies. Although it isn't easy to understand this country at all: the richest and most powerful country in the world lives, at least in its biggest city, with such a degree of rot, violence, pure sickness, madness, extreme variance on every level, that it often takes your breath away.'[3]

Did Habermas see *Chelsea Girls*, Andy Warhol's six-hour experimental film about the residents of the Chelsea Hotel? Did he read Joan Didion's piece in the *Saturday Evening Post* about the Californian hippies, whose first sentence, 'The centre is not holding', confirmed that William Butler Yeats's worst fears, written in the dark hour of 1919, were the new American reality? There is no doubt that Habermas was interested in the civil rights movement, which was at its zenith then, shortly before the assassination of Martin Luther King. As he had said to a colleague before his departure for New York, the Meyersohns' apartment 'even' came with a 'Black domestic'. Did the employment of such a domestic worker become a moral problem for the Habermas family, as it did for other members of New York's liberal middle class? We can only speculate. The following year, Habermas analysed the 'race conflict' in the USA from a Marxist perspective at an academic symposium on the Yugoslavian island of Korčula. Since 'deprived groups are not social classes' whose exploitation is necessary for capitalist society today, their protest could lead to conditions resembling those of civil war, but had no revolutionary potential.[4]

What is certain is that Habermas saw little of pop culture, which, according to its historian Warhol, peaked that year in

New York. In this, Habermas was a true follower of Adorno. Even the new Beatles album that electrified Manhattan in the summer of 1967, *Sgt. Pepper*, seems to have left no mark on him. Years later, when Peter Handke asked him at a party at Siegfried Unseld's what he thought of the Beatles, Habermas had to admit he was not familiar with their work. Whereupon the Beatles fan Handke allegedly began beating him. But, after all, even the fisticuffs of the pop-culturally savvy writer reveal the backwardness of the German culture industry. If we may believe Warhol, the Abstract Expressionists were the last New York bohemians to settle their disputes physically: 'They were always exploding and having fist fights about their work and their love lives.' But the 1960s brought camp and pop, and with them a queer, playful sensitivity that set the tone of the new avant-gardes – in contrast to the masculine Suhrkamp culture, in which someone always seems to have been fighting with someone. According to Ute Habermas, spontaneously rolling her eyes as the subject comes up, that went on until the 1980s.[5]

To the Habermases, Frankfurt had once represented the whole wide world, but after their return from New York, it felt like a provincial capital. That was one reason why the lecture tours, visiting professorships and fellowships that Habermas now took almost yearly became a fixed feature of his life. In 1975, Hannah Arendt tried to recruit him as her successor at the New School; in the early 1980s he was sought by the University of California at Berkeley. As he has intimated on various occasions, he felt more appreciated by the Americans than by his own compatriots. Which raises the question why he didn't accept one of those tempting offers. There are many possible reasons: the institute in Starnberg, consideration for his family, the social life in the Suhrkamp cultural milieu. An Ivy League professorship would no doubt have been the cherry on top of his academic career. But, at a time when physical location still made a difference in intellectual life, he would have had to give up his role as a public intellectual, which necessarily depended on access to the German public sphere. Did Habermas need the limelight, in spite of all protestations to the contrary, or was he held back by a feeling of responsibility for the political culture of his country? The journalist Arno Widmann, who has observed him over many years, believes 'that he thought, in fact he *knew*, he was needed more here'.[6]

# Running the Gauntlet in Frankfurt

In fact, people were waiting to hear his voice in Frankfurt in 1968. His colleague Dieter Henrich once said Habermas could have been 'the charismatic leader of the student movement'. Joschka Fischer, the future Green Party leader and foreign minister who began attending his classes sporadically in the 1968/69 winter term, remembers overfilled Habermas seminars in which the leading socialist student activists, 'all the SDS celebrities', were present – although, by this time, relations between the activists and the professor were already tense. Adorno having shied away from political praxis, the students turned to his younger colleague, who protested against the Vietnam War, the Social Democrats' formation of a 'Grand Coalition' government with the Christian Democrats, and the subsequent adoption of the *Notstandsgesetze*, a constitutional amendment that would curtail civil rights in case of a national emergency. But Habermas too, sympathizing more with moderate forces than with anti-authoritarian radicals, was unable to fulfil the students' expectations. He believed, as he phrased it in retrospect, 'rather in the reformability of schools and universities than in total revolution, or in the total immovability of an ossified whole, which amounted to the same thing'. From the 1960s on, if not before, he saw it as his duty to criticize the West German state from within.[1]

As early as the spring of 1967, Jacob Taubes hinted in a letter to Hans Robert Jauss, a Romance philologist at the University of Constance, that Habermas was an unwilling champion of the rebels: 'Even the strongest nerves are worn down by running the gauntlet in Frankfurt, where the sociology students, radicalized by Adorno's theory and disappointed by Adorno's practice, demand from the younger generation what Horkheimer and Adorno always promised but never delivered – with compound interest.' A week later, the pacifist student Benno Ohnesorg was shot by police at a demonstration against the Shah of Iran's visit to Berlin, and his funeral procession of 7,000 in Hanover was immediately followed by the symposium on 'University and Democracy' where the student movement leader Rudi Dutschke proposed opposing 'state terrorism' with a strategy of direct action. Habermas, speaking after Dutschke, warned against 'left Fascism'. In spite of his subsequent defence – he had been referring not to the Nazis, but to the Italian left-wing Fascists of the 1920s – Habermas could not rid himself after that of the reputation of being a liberal – more precisely, a '*Scheissliberaler*'. While his assistant Oskar Negt analysed the degeneration of his left-liberal consciousness, the emigrant poet Erich Fried in London asked him to withdraw his judgement because it played into the enemy's hands: 'I believe it has happened to every single one of us that we have said something in anger that missed its effect because it fit in a pre-moulded vocabulary that we are actually fighting against.' Ten years later, during the 'German Autumn' of domestic left-wing terrorism, Habermas himself characterized his phrase as an 'overreaction'.[2]

In the course of the year that followed, while the tone of the debate was escalating both among the student protesters and in the tabloid press, the mutual alienation between Habermas and the rebels solidified. In September 1967, at the

Socialist German Students' League conference, Dutschke, along with his comrade Hans-Jürgen Krahl, for the first time advocated the formation of an urban guerrilla movement. Six months later, on 11 April 1968, Dutschke was shot by the self-proclaimed anti-Communist and *National-Zeitung* reader Josef Bachmann. In early June, after file cabinets had been broken open during the recent occupation of the Frankfurt university, Habermas, back from his semester in New York, spoke in the dining-hall on the 'Pseudo-revolution and Its Children'. Although he found the 'new demonstration techniques' to be 'outstandingly suitable' as ways to penetrate the 'niches' of the 'bureaucratic power structure' and to oppose the 'functionally necessary depoliticization of broad segments of the population' by mass education, his assessment of the students' theoretical weapons was scathing. Marx's theory, debatable in itself, had been broken down to a 'handy format of platitudes', and now aroused revolutionary expectations. But those expectations were illusory: 'All, absolutely all of the generally accepted signs of a revolutionary situation are lacking'; those who acted as revolutionaries under such conditions, he said, were simply labouring under a 'delusion'. Habermas recommended the students assess the situation realistically and seek the help of public intellectuals and union representatives who had experience with the media.[3]

As much as he welcomed the new forms of protest in principle, Habermas seems to have felt they were out of place in his own classes, where the atmosphere had grown more confrontational after his accusation of 'left Fascism'. Even in his inaugural lecture, anticipating his later theory of communication, he had sketched the ideal of a 'non-authoritarian and universally practised dialogue' between everyone and everyone, an ideal that was implicit in every speech act as 'anticipating the realization of the good life'. But students who misunderstood this as an invitation to challenge his authority as the instructor of a seminar discovered that he was not

open to experiments in cultural revolution. 'I naively assumed
that you would agree to the diminution of your authority',
explained Gerhard Stamer, a doctoral candidate who had
evidently answered Habermas's interpretations of Hegel and
Marx with insubordinate criticism. He had intended by his
provocation to 'break with fossilized forms of discussion and
bring about a lively, anxiety-free communication'. His reli-
ance on Habermas's 'generosity' turned out to be a mistake,
however. Forty years later, Joschka Fischer, who had attended
the same seminar, remembered an 'academic execution' that
consisted in Habermas tearing apart the student's arguments
'sentence by sentence': 'There was nothing friendly about it.'
Fischer also felt, however, that being taken that seriously by
their professor was the highest form of recognition.[4]

That much is true: Habermas's inability to engage in breezy
talk, his propensity to take the other person's position literally
in all its ramifications and with all its consequences – often far
beyond those intended – is truly remarkable. Thrashing out
an argument with him, as Oskar Negt knew from experience,
required 'an enormous justificatory effort'. But the impression
is equally hard to resist that his boundless capacity for discussion comes with a downside: a lack of generosity, a mistrust,
and a touchiness that sometimes undermines it. 'A surprising
number of conflicts for a scholar working so calmly', wrote
Urs Jaeggi in the early 1980s. 'He is, as his reactions show,
easily irritable; he reacts sensitively, and tends to see himself
as stigmatized. Does this make him solitary, capable of real
dialogue only with a few people?'[5]

On the other hand, perhaps observations like this one are
based on the misunderstanding that Habermas is interested in
discussion for the sake of discussion. As the countless public
debates in which he has been involved over the course of
his life indicate, he discusses in order to advance his positions. This brings with it a well-developed awareness of the
enemy's movements. In any case, he never suffered from the

'incapacity for opposition' that Arnold Gehlen saw in his modern contemporaries – if anything, to take a term from Odo Marquard, then from an 'antagonization compulsion'. As Gehlen discovered, the theorist of dominance-free discourse did not exactly handle his opponents with kid gloves. After Habermas, writing in *Merkur*, had panned Gehlen's polemic against '68, *Moral und Hypermoral*, as the 'political stock in trade of an out-of-step intellectual of the Right', his victim never wrote a word again in that magazine. According to the sociologist Heinz Bude, although Habermas considered the theorist of enmity, Carl Schmitt, to be the embodiment of German anti-culture, he himself was 'Schmittian' in his own communicative practice. He has maintained his propensity to confrontation and polemics to this day. Although one might have suspected otherwise, Habermas has never been caught wanting 'to engage the right in dialogue' – on the contrary: the public sphere must tolerate 'robust demonstrations' and even 'heated forms of conflict', as he explained in a 2020 interview. 'I have absolutely no sympathy with the notion that we should kowtow to enraged citizens [*Wutbürger*].'[6]

'For almost a decade, the publisher Suhrkamp has been setting little time bombs, which are now "exploding" in the universities': thus Jacob Taubes described the role of the influential publishing house towards the end of the 1960s. In autumn of 1968, the publishing company itself was rocked by a silent explosion. The assembled editors submitted a declaration to their boss Siegfried Unseld, in which they disavowed his decision-making power as publisher and demanded an equal say. That was presented as just the first step on the road to an expropriation of the literary means of production. Unseld not only took offence personally, but saw his life's work endangered, and he sought support among his authors. He might well expect solidarity from that quarter, because the charter proposed by the rebelling editors accorded the authors no significant rights at all. Martin Walser found the initiative simply ridiculous. Adorno, citing Marx, assured Unseld that the editors' demands were unjustified – but preferred to keep a low profile. In the decisive meeting with the insurgents, which went on until well after midnight, Habermas leapt into the breach for his publisher. 'He prefaced his statement very thoroughly,' Unseld writes in his 'Chronicles', 'and with his full theoretical armament presented the thesis that it made no sense to subject a publishing house which was already bringing out the right progressive literature, which was working well on the whole, in which the authors as productive workers were satisfied overall and in detail, to an experiment which put at risk all the influence that the house currently had.'[7]

Does Habermas's intervention constitute a case of communicative action, or was it strategic action? To Unseld, it was essentially a pragmatic argument: until the ownership relations of the overall society were changed, it made no sense to overturn the very publishing company that was more devoted to such change than any other. Habermas's 'comprehensive lecture' had a paralysing effect on the editors, which may have been his intention: 'We, the editors, understood', one of them recalled, 'our "just cause" was not just: our attempt to risk more democracy within the publishing house was obviously incommensurable with the free capitalist constitutional order ... and it had failed – not even with aplomb. Silently, we went our separate ways.' The mood was so depressed that no one even hung around for a last cigarette.[8]

As Unseld's 'Chronicles' recount, the editors surrendered without much resistance. While some of them, including Karl Markus Michel, to Habermas's chagrin, tendered their resignations, the others were willing to go on working for the capitalist publisher Suhrkamp. To Unseld, who was now in 'constant telephone contact' with Habermas, the philosopher must have been a more important ally than ever after this episode.[9]

# Rocket Science for a
# Better Society

The philosophical moves that Habermas made up to the dawn of the 1970s can be understood as a search for an escape from the subjective philosophy that would take him from the idea of 'awareness' [*Vernehmen*], as he had found it in Heidegger and Schelling, to the concept of 'understanding' [*Verständigung*] that he later developed in his theory of communication. Driven by an insatiable appetite for reading, he traversed a broad, bewildering terrain in those years which was difficult even for contemporary observers to reconnoitre. Leo Strauss, the political theorist at the University of Chicago to whom Habermas sent a copy of his collected essays, *Theorie und Praxis*, in 1964, was full of praise for his young colleague's acumen, but at the same time remarked to Karl Löwith that the foundations of Habermas's philosophical standpoint were 'utterly baffling'. He was without a doubt a representative of Western Marxism and, like other Western Marxists, he arrived at early Hegelian positions via a subtle critique of Marx, expanding the perspective of labour to include that of interaction, and the issue of material exploitation to include that of mutual recognition among legal subjects in a bourgeois society. At the same time, however, Habermas discussed widely varying approaches, including

American pragmatism, German theory of the state, psycho-analysis and the philosophical anthropology of Arnold Gehlen and Habermas's PhD supervisor Erich Rothacker. Since the mid-1960s, he had been working to place the normative claims of Critical Theory on a firm scientific foundation by means of an anthropology of cognitive interests.[1]

In *Knowledge and Human Interests*, the book that grew out of his inaugural lecture in Frankfurt and was published in 1968 in Suhrkamp's white-covered *Theorie* series, Habermas distinguished three viewpoints, or rather three 'knowledge-constitutive interests', 'from which we can apprehend reality as such in any way whatsoever': the interest in technical 'control' over the forces of nature, which is the foundation of the experimental natural sciences; the interest in 'mutual understanding', which is the origin of the hermeneutic social sciences; and, finally, the interest in 'emancipation from the compulsion of internal nature', a way of knowledge of the world with equally deep roots in the *conditio humana* that Habermas associated with the 'critical social science[s]'. The function of the latter sciences consists in freeing the subject by a process of self-reflection 'from dependence on hypostasized powers'. Emancipation as a methodically controlled process of knowledge: although *Knowledge and Human Interests* is a fundamental critique of positivism, it must be seen itself as a document of the belief, typical of the times, in what Habermas called the 'weightiest of productive forces' in modern society – namely, science.[2]

Although he had never lain on the couch himself, Habermas imagined psychoanalysis as a blueprint for the critical social sciences. His first exposure to psychoanalysis, shortly after he joined the Institute for Social Research, was at a 1956 sympo-sium for Freud's 100th birthday. Hans Magnus Enzensberger had long been courting Habermas as the 'ideal' author for his journal *Kursbuch* ('from the point of view of both qualifica-tions and style'), and, in 1967, Habermas proposed an issue on psychoanalysis: 'Because psychoanalysis is being beset by the exact sciences, especially in America but also elsewhere, and is increasingly being forced into the obscure role of a therapeutic art, it seems a good idea to me to demonstrate by this example what a critical science could be.' With his professorial thoroughness, Habermas made the mistake of including a complete table of contents for the proposed issue, including the authors to be solicited. At a time when every periodical in the country was competing for Habermas's collaboration, Enzensberger had no qualms about gently rebuffing him. In regard to both content and form, the exposé was too homogeneous and premeditated – good for an anthology, but not for a periodical. Furthermore, in the margin of his letter, Habermas had unguardedly hinted at an alternative: an issue on 'planning'. 'this alternative, i confess,' Enzensberger replied in his idiosyncratic lower case, 'captivates me straight away. i think the topic is, not more important, but more urgent.'[3]

Although Habermas's reply was somewhat thin-lipped, he does not seem to have resented the poet's rejection. If only because of his 'own repressed history of journalism', he looked forward to submitting a new proposal in the future. Soon after that, though, the student revolt escalated, the *Kursbuch* took up a position in its vanguard, and Enzensberger slipped into the role of a 'Harlequin in the court of the pseudo-revolutionaries', fancying himself egging on the irresponsible playground revolution – according to Habermas, at least, who from then on viewed Enzensberger with suspicion as a seismographer of the zeitgeist. Whatever the reasons may have been, although Enzensberger approached him later, Habermas never published an article in the *Kursbuch*.[4]

The demonstration of the critical potential of psychoanalysis that Habermas had proposed to the journal was ultimately reserved for the closing section of *Knowledge and Human Interests*, which quickly rose in the ranks of Suhrkamp's classic titles the following year. Unlike hermeneutics, which exposed the buried meaning of historic documents, the therapeutic practice of psychoanalysis was aimed at initiating a process of self-reflection that would enable the patient to regain 'a portion of lost life history'. Habermas said in this connection that 'reflective insight' should permit the 'continuation . . . of an interrupted, neurotically-inhibited process of formation of the self'. Translating this understanding of therapeutic practice from neurotic individuals to the society as a whole, he recommended it as a model for an epistemologically grounded critique of ideology.[5]

But what could it signify for a society such as Germany's after Nazism to reclaim its repressed history? With regard to West Germany in 1968, this question cannot be answered without reference to Alexander and Margarete Mitscherlich and their study published the previous year, *The Inability to Mourn: Principles of Collective Behaviour.* Many readings have neglected the central thesis of that book: namely, the finding that Germans' repression, diagnosed in the title, is focused not on the murder victims, but on the beloved 'Führer'. The Mitscherlichs were all the more successful in establishing the Freudian term 'grief work' as a paradigm, and psychoanalysis as the key theoretical framework in the German discipline of *Vergangenheitsbewältigung*, 'coming to grips with the past'. This constellation was also beneficial to the reception of *Knowledge and Human Interests.* In the preface of his book, Habermas paid homage to Alexander Mitscherlich, with whom he had been friends since his time in Heidelberg. However, all references to the Germans' 'lost life history' remained implicit in his text.[6]

At our meeting, Habermas proves a virtuoso of understatement, taking great pains to dispel all suspicions of special talents, to say nothing of genius. Thus he attributes the no fewer than eleven professorships that were offered him in the course of his career not so much to any personal merit as to the growth surge in universities that accompanied Germany's 'education offensive' in the 1960s: just as he had finished his habilitation, there was 'a flood of appointments'. And in fact it is hard to resist the impression that he was always in the right place at the right time – the strange feeling of a pre-established harmony between his lifetime and cosmic time. In 1964, the year in which the student movement got underway, he returned to Frankfurt as Horkheimer's successor – only to go back underground in the provinces when the time was right, seven years later, as director of the Max Planck Institute for the Study of the Scientific and Technical World. In the Frankfurt of 1971, Habermas's decision to go to Starnberg was a political issue. *Der Spiegel* reported that, in order to work on his theory undisturbed by teaching obligations, Habermas was retreating 'into a kind of German art nouveau version of Oxford': this was an allusion to the posh building in which the Max Planck Society had rented space. A Frankfurt student newspaper meanwhile accused him of betraying the project of a critical university, which had just begun to take institutional shape through his contributions to the new Hessian Act on Higher Education. Herbert Marcuse was more understanding about Habermas's departure, but felt it was 'a "symbolic act" which is part of the end of the Frankfurt School'.[7]

Left-wing academics pursued the art of surviving the 1970s without damaging their reputations, their integrity and their intellectual freshness. Habermas managed it quite a bit better than many of his contemporaries. As the protest movement gave way to the plethora of subcultures, as the outlook dark-ened with the end of the postwar boom and the opponents of '68 proclaimed a new course, Habermas disappeared from the scene, analysing the crisis of late capitalism and writing his grand social theory from the safe distance of Upper Bavaria. Among the staff at the Max Planck Institute, there was an expectation that they would be distilling the legacy of the student movement into its 'academically usable' components. Heinz Bude, then a sociology student, nurtured the idea of building a kind of German RAND Corporation in Starnberg, after the Californian model. And it is not an exaggeration to say that the Institute with the long name, already a fossil by the 1980s, was the high point of the project of deriving another universal, political–normative orientation from the accumulated findings of the different academic disciplines – a think tank for left-wing fundamental research, for grand interdisciplinary synthesis: rocket science for a better society.[8]

The founding director of the Institute, Carl Friedrich von Weizsäcker, had been a living incarnation of that programme with his idiosyncratic range of interests, from conflict prevention to the theory of science and quantum mechanics. The Max Planck Society no doubt intended it thus, following the principle that scientific institutes ought to be organized around the research profiles of their directors. But didn't that lend new legitimacy to the figure of the 'master thinker' – a figure that Weizsäcker's new co-director Habermas considered both atavistic and politically suspect since his break with Heidegger? It is conspicuous at least that Habermas, in his 1971 survey of German postwar philosophy – 'Why More Philosophy?' – advocated 'depersonalizing' his discipline and subjecting it to the logic of the scientific division of labour. The age of charismatic masters was coming to an end even in the backward German academic scene: in this opinion, Habermas anticipated the anonymous 'network' and 'cluster' research of today's grant-driven university.[9]

The studies that Weizsäcker directed in his department fell under the rubric of 'future research', a discipline that he, as a kind of West German Oppenheimer, had founded in the 1960s, together with Robert Jungk and other critical scientists and diagnosticians of the present, in response to the danger of nuclear war. Thus his interest in bringing Habermas to the Institute may have been heightened by the fact that the younger man's theoretical orientation also had futuristic traits. The theory of late capitalism that Habermas was working on at that time was aimed at predicting future crises in the Western social welfare states. In his mid-1970s reconstruction of historical materialism – a theory of evolution of modern society – he formulated the general ambition of understanding enough to make 'conditioned predictions of events that will occur in the future'. The editors of the German edition of *Playboy* magazine, launched in 1972 in Munich, seem to have taken him at his word: in 1974, they asked him what he thought would be the dominant issue of 'the next 25 years' – a period that seems astronomically long for prognoses in the social sciences today, even discounting climate change.[10]

At this point, some thought must be given to the expectations of the petroleum-based democracies of the postwar decades. In the spaciousness of their open-ended future, the starkest contradictions of the advanced capitalist societies could conceivably be reconciled: whether avant-garde and culture industry, fast cars and welfare states, or highbrow entertainment and the theory of modern society. The promise of future participation that lends Western societies their legitimacy was also able to lend a progressive, even an emancipatory touch to the brave new world that *Playboy* promised its readers. It was no coincidence that the magazine's logo, the *Playboy* bunny, faced left; the US edition featured Muhammad Ali, Malcolm X and John Lennon. Marshall McLuhan predicted the end of the Gutenberg galaxy in its pages, and soon afterwards Leslie Fiedler heralded the postmodern era. Even the 'septuagenarian superstar of the revolutionaries', Habermas's friend Herbert Marcuse, was the object of a six-page portrait in *Playboy* in 1970.[11]

Aside from fundamental reservations, Habermas's failure to reply to the magazine's request may have had to do with the fact that *Playboy* had approached him a crucial moment too late. In the aftermath of the oil crisis and 'stagflation', as the optimistic Keynesian planners grew increasingly perplexed, the sense of time in Western societies was changing. It soon transpired that shrinking expectations themselves were one of the most serious symptoms of the crisis that Habermas had undertaken to analyse. It stands to reason that this necessarily had a feedback effect on the theory under development. The belief in the predictive power of speculative thinking was still strong, but, as Habermas stated some years later, bad times were already dawning for 'attempts at orientation directed towards the future'. Weizsäcker's futurology too declined in appeal in the course of the 1970s. And even the enthusiastic Marcuse had replied with resignation to the *Playboy* interviewer's question about his future plans: 'Who can plan anything any more?'[12]

The recollections of former Starnberg staff members are inconsistent. Habermas seems to have been a sociable person to work for, never dodging a round of drinks, yet at the same time he preferred to write his own books rather than participate in his research groups' discussions. He was really 'the old-fashioned type of the scholar working away in solitude', he confessed to one colleague. If he felt his responsibility for his staff to be rather an imposition, that may explain the stories of paralysing rivalry and humiliating rebukes in his department. While Weizsäcker experimented – perhaps really following the model of the RAND Corporation – with flexible forms of working, Habermas pressed for the nine-to-five. Weizsäcker later explained that he had recruited Habermas to give the militant leftists in his institute a 'well-established left-wing director' who 'would at last impose *law and order* on them'. He had apparently sized up his new co-director better than the Frankfurt students who had tried to incite him to cultural revolution in his seminar, only to discover, like the Suhrkamp editors, that he was not one to 'embark on adventures', as he himself once put it.[13]

# What We Must Presuppose

Immersing oneself in Habermas's *œuvre* for a long time means becoming familiar with an unwieldy vocabulary that runs like a leitmotif through his writings, along with its various turns and transformations. That vocabulary includes comparatively unspecific terms such as 'rationalization', 'learning process' and 'public sphere', characteristic verbs such as 'deliver' [*entbinden*], 'become liquid' or 'aflow' [*verflüssigen*] and 'reconstruct after the fact' [*nachrekonstruieren*] – and, not least, the discursive markers of the Habermasian world, such as 'cognitive interest', the 'colonization of the lifeworld' and 'constitutional patriotism'. But his best-known neologisms may still be – outside the specialist world of philosophy, at least – the terms 'dominance-free discourse' and the 'ideal speech situation', which advanced to the foreground of his texts in the late 1960s as, in search of a firm scientific foundation for his vision of a 'friendly living together' after his excursions to Marx and psychoanalysis, he finally found his Archimedean point in language or, more precisely, communication. In order to speak meaningfully to one another – in Habermas's both fundamental and far-reaching realization – we must presuppose, counterfactually as the case may be, that mutual understanding [*Verständigung*] and everything that goes with it, such as truth, authenticity and justice, can in principle be achieved by means of language. We must pretend, at least when we step out of our everyday interactions and into an explanatory argumentation, that we are dealing with equal, earnest, reasonable, more or less self-aware partners who can readily justify their positions and preferences and are equally willing to listen to our reasons. Language itself compels us to presuppose a 'dominance-free discourse' or, as Habermas called it then, following the English-language speech act theory, an 'ideal speech situation' in which such factors as dominance and influence are neutralized, and which is ruled only by the 'curiously coercion-free force of the better argument'.[1]

Did he ever wish he had never brought this concept into the world? For whatever reason, the 'ideal speech situation' has not merited an entry of its own in the *Habermas Handbook*, and in a 2018 interview, the philosopher stressed that he had not used that 'misleading expression' since 1972 – probably because he realized early on that it exposed a vulnerability to his critics. For the spirit of the 'ideal speech situation' was that of the utopian Old Left. When Habermas spoke of 'anticipating the realization of the good life' or, more explicitly, of a 'form of life to be realized in the future', his liberal-conservative critics said he seemed to be thinking of a new, redeemed humankind, but one in which the classless society of Marxist tradition was replaced by an ideal community of communication.[2]

The Catholic philosopher Robert Spaemann, who had kept in touch with Habermas since their time together in Heidelberg, exposed the 'anarchistic' core of Habermas's theory of communicative action. Making the legitimacy of a political commonwealth dependent on an uncoerced, universal consensus meant misunderstanding the nature of the political, which is characterized not by scholarly discourse, but by conflicts of interest, strategic deliberation and dilemma – in a word, by the phenomenon of power. Habermas's fallacy,

Spaemann found, was that, with the overconfidence that is typical of intellectuals, he mistook the interactive situation of his seminars for that of society as a whole: 'A space for non-coercive discourse is vital for society. But that space is the "school", not the "city" in the sense of the polis.'[3]

Ralf Dahrendorf too, who in his own theory emphasized the socially constructive power of political conflicts, saw the ideal of an uncoerced consensus as the 'dream of a better world' that dated back to Rousseau and was not compatible with a liberal political organization. Dieter Henrich found that Habermas's 'Rousseauism drunk on language' went so far as to express the utopian hope of redeeming the alienated subject in a communicative community. Niklas Luhmann, on the other hand, in the competing social theory of communication that he developed in the 1970s, focused not so much on the political implications as on the descriptive accuracy of Habermas's approach. He posed the rhetorical question whether the idea of exchanging rational arguments with a view to mutual understanding overlooked the dynamics of actually observable discussions, with their time limitations, their 'scare words' and other 'terrestrial' defects. Michel Foucault, the theorist of power relations, raised similar objections: 'The idea that there could exist a state of communication that would allow games of truth to circulate freely, without any constraints or coercive effects, seems utopian to me', he explained in an interview shortly before his death.[4]

That was the line of criticism that I too adopted in the 1990s: a theory that disqualified a large part of the communication that in fact occurred in the world as deficient, inadequate, 'distorted', clearly lacked some grounding in reality. But I seem not to have read Habermas very carefully back then, otherwise I would have noticed one attempt after another to make his 'vocabulary of the as-if' more precise. 'For every possible communication, the anticipation of the ideal speech situation has the significance of a constitutive illusion that is at the same time the prefiguration of a form of life', he wrote in the 1969 seminar paper in which the concept first appeared – and this sentence tacitly blurs an important distinction. If we conceive of the ideal speech situation as a 'constitutive illusion', then it is a necessary presupposition, that is, one that obtains whenever we speak. If, on the other hand, we call it the 'prefiguration of a form of life', then it must stand for a future society to be brought about. In philosophical terminology, the concept invoked is in the one case transcendental, Kantian, and in the other dialectical, Hegelian-Marxian. The accusation that Robert Spaemann aimed at Habermas is, essentially, that he did not distinguish sufficiently between the two senses of the concept – and that he perhaps wanted to keep both possibilities open.[5]

Since then, Habermas has unequivocally committed himself to the transcendental interpretation. 'To the extent to which it suggests a concrete form of life, even the expression "the ideal speech situation" is misleading', he wrote in 1984, when he had parted for good with the theoretical framework of Marxism. Ten years later, he termed the expression a 'fallacy of misplaced concreteness', because it suggests 'a final stage which can be realized in time, and this cannot be what is meant'. That doesn't mean that he had abandoned the complex idea of a counterfactual presupposition per se – one might also say, of the social effectiveness of subjective claims to validity: he still saw it as 'the nerve of my entire theoretical undertaking'. But he did everything he could to free it from its diffuse utopian excesses. 'It's really quite simple', he explained in the early 1990s: 'whenever we mean what we say, we raise the claim that what is said is true, or right, or truthful. With this claim, a small bit of ideality breaks into our everyday lives.' By this time, Habermas had long since abandoned the terms 'ideal speech situation' and 'dominance-free discourse'. More cautiously, he spoke instead of 'idealizations' or 'counterfactual presuppositions' – and of 'deliberation' generally. The disarmament of his terminology went hand in hand with the narrowing of his theoretical project. After he had left Starnberg to return to the University of Frankfurt, he toned down his ambition to explain the foundations of social organization, limiting his focus to a philosophy of constitutional democracy. A certain satisfaction seems to be audible in the sociologist Dahrendorf's comment that Habermas's 'greatest project' had failed.[6]

As a busy botanist, Habermas had arranged many flowers in his theory of communicative action: J. L. Austin's speech act theory, Gadamer's hermeneutics, Luhmann's systems theory – and of course the idea of the 'talking cure', which he adapted from Karl Jaspers and psychoanalysis. But his thinking would probably never have made such a splash if it had not also referred to the non-academic zeitgeist. As he once remarked himself, 'when it formulates its problems and when it has an effect on the public at large, philosophy draws from the same sources'. Habermas, who approvingly quotes Hegel's saying about reading the newspaper being a 'realist's morning prayer', can be pictured as an impassioned participant in the present.[7]

In any case, his theory seems tailor-made to fit the Bonn Republic. The Germans only learned to appreciate the cultural technique of discussion after the debacle of 1945. While Western Europeans had accustomed themselves over centuries to more and more civilized social mores, the Germans had never stopped cultivating the authoritarian virtues of the paternalistic state. *Kompromiss*, 'compromise', was a dirty word in German up until 1945, always understood to be a 'sham': *fauler Kompromiss*. It took the unconditional surrender and American re-education to make the achievement of discursive communication take root in Germany. The round tables and the discussion formats that were so typical of cultural life in the early West Germany can be seen as the school of communicative action. The journalist Eugen Kogon, for example, introduced a radio discussion with Horkheimer and Adorno in 1950 with the self-reflective remark that life in the 'administrated world' – the topic of the broadcast – suffered from constant time pressure. In just fifteen minutes, in fact, Horkheimer was supposed to be in Bad Nauheim! 'And so here we sit: trembling, nervous, because we have other appointments ahead of us.' Under such conditions, it was impossible, he said, to have a 'calm, thorough and reasonable' discussion. 'For my part, at any rate, I am going to pretend I have all the time in the world. And I think that this as-if can become a reality.' It sounds as if Kogon had read Habermas and summarized his crucial idea for his listeners. But that is impossible, because at that time, at the beginning of the 1950s, Habermas himself was still busy with Heidegger's ideas.[8]

Even a decade later, the rebelling students' neologism *ausdiskutieren*, roughly 'to elucidate completely by exhaustive discussion', basically expressed a counterfactual presupposition: in the counterculture's rural communes, grassroots groups and collective enterprises, the practice of 'talking things through' became an end in itself. Habermas, who on a variety of occasions described himself as a 'product of re-education', made the 'unforced force of the better argument' into the cornerstone of his monumental social theory. Adorno before him, who said nothing could be right in a life that was wrong, had praised the West German state as a 'historical breathing space' in which he found urgently needed time to think. His disciple went far beyond this cautious diagnosis and suspected that the older proponents of Critical Theory 'never took' the achievements of liberal democracy 'very seriously'. As he grew older, Habermas was inclined to see West Germany as an historic success story. 'For the first time in centuries', Germany had managed to 'become a contemporary of Western Europe': this was a 'great intellectual accomplishment', which he regarded as an achievement of his generation. And in fact, the role of the philosophical pioneer in this process, conferring the blessings of a philosophical system on the belated civilization of his countrymen, fell to him.[9]

# The Stigma of the Spoken

In her essay 'Truth and Politics', published in *The New Yorker* in 1967, Hannah Arendt writes that, in the modern age, after the loss of the great metaphysical certainties, the abstract truths of philosophy need to be in some way attested, witnessed, by their authors. Habermas too once remarked that every philosophy has an 'open side upon which it must be complemented and proven, so to speak, by the actual and everyday existence of the philosopher'.[1] Just look around in the recent history of philosophy: the special fascination that figures such as Nietzsche, Wittgenstein and Arendt continue to exert has a great deal to do with the fact that there seems to be an unbreakable link between their ideas and their lives. Philosophy *professors*, on the other hand – who have been the official representatives of philosophy at least since the turn of the nineteenth century, when the field metamorphosed into an academic discipline – are suspected, outside the ivory tower, of practising an irrelevant, bureaucratic, inauthentic thinking. Hardly anyone was more strongly suspected in this regard than Habermas. As a father, a homeowner and a career academic who, unlike other philosophy professors such as Heidegger or Foucault, not only refrained from taking any anti-academic pose but, on the contrary, made it his agenda to advance the scientific character of his field, Habermas seems to be the epitome of the university philosopher – and his philosophy looks like a professional enterprise that lacks a personal witness. Naturally there is the existential caesura of 1945, to which he has referred repeatedly, but that is, first of all, a societal narrative, not an individual one, and, second, it is a narrative about the good fortune of being *spared* by the course of history.

Has this elusiveness contributed to the covert exegesis that winds around Habermas's congenital anomaly? Even at the risk of crude kitchen-psychological speculation, it is tempting to see his philosophy as somehow related to his speech defect. In an early version of his theory of communication, smuggled into his scathing 1970 review of Arnold Gehlen's theory of morals, Habermas wrote: 'Being human is the fearlessness ultimately left to us once we have had the insight that only the perilous means of an ever-so-fragile communication can resist the dangers of a universal fragility.'[2] That communication is 'fragile', that its success can never be taken for granted – is this something he learned from personal experience? Was it his own difficulty in making himself understood that made communication a universal problem for him?

Habermas's own remarks on this subject are few and far between. When he mentioned it at all, he merely alluded to the existence of 'very personal experiences' that gave his confidence in social relations a 'profoundly ambivalent' tinge. Only once, in his speech on accepting the Kyoto Prize in 2004, did he comment explicitly on his cleft palate, acceding with tangible reluctance to the organizers' request for autobiographical remarks. The lives of philosophers are not suitable material for hagiography, he said. Moreover, the kind of publicity he was interested in was concerned with the 'exchange of reasons and opinions' and not the 'self-presentation' of celebrities. After these preliminary qualifying remarks, however, the laureate was willing after all to talk about the 'biographical roots' of the topic of his life's work, his 'obsession' with communication in the public sphere. He hinted that the ideas of philosophers, or at least the 'less original' among them, are often 'nothing more than an expression of the biography out of which they arise' – a surprising biographical thesis for him, but one that also displays the characteristic Habermasian modesty: the dismissal of any suppositions of genius.[3]

The degree of abstraction of his acceptance speech is a further indication that he was merely fulfilling an obligation. We can only guess what painful experiences were involved in the operations he had to undergo in his childhood, and in the 'difficulties' at school that he mentions – and what existential danger, in the climate of a political system in which a cleft palate, along with the conditions then known as 'clubfoot' and 'lunacy', was listed as a danger to the 'racial hygiene'. Habermas quickly gets around to his real topic, the influence of his disability on his philosophical interests – and he underscores the speculative nature of such inferences by phrasing the entire theme in the conditional. It may well be that his childhood surgical treatments awakened his sensitivity to people's mutual dependency; that the experience of being unable to make himself understood because of a speech impediment sparked his interest in communication; that the insults and discrimination of his classmates sensitized him to 'the peculiar vulnerability of socialized individuals'. 'Only in a failing performance does the medium of linguistic communication emerge as a shared stratum without which we could not exist as individuals'; in other words, only where communication is distorted can the utopia of an ideal speech situation arise.[4]

Could that mean Habermas's 'less original' ideas crystallized around an idiosyncratic kernel? May we see them as a rationalization of his speech impediment? He almost seems to make that suggestion when, later in his speech, he mentions his preference for written language. All his life, he says, he was persuaded 'of the superiority of the written word': a person who writes 'disguises the stigma of the spoken'. In fact, a preference for writing is one of the running themes of his biography. From his student days, Habermas drew less attention to himself by original comments in seminars than by his talent for writing. Thanks to the good fortune of being in the right place at the right time, he seemed to establish himself effortlessly as a freelance contributor in the rapidly growing West German press. The same is true of many other ambitious young men (and a few young women) of his generation. But in one respect, he has a special status among the 'media intellectuals' of early West Germany. Unlike others of his age, such as Enzensberger or Walser, who splashed about in the salubrious waters of the public broadcasting networks, Habermas almost never ventured into radio, much less television. Even as a leftist professor who played the lecture halls of 1968, he was never what you could call a stage hog. Shying away from the cameras and microphones of the mass media, he withdrew whenever possible 'to the precision afforded by expressing myself in the written form'. He needed 'paper in front of me, blank paper', to attain the satisfaction of philosophy. When a London producer tried to recruit him in 1973 for a discussion on British television with his famous New York acquaintance Hannah Arendt, he declined. In fact, he recounted, he had only appeared before television cameras once in his whole life. 'You may consider it a personal idiosyncrasy of mine that I have reservations about the screen.'[5]

But to return to the speech Habermas gave in Kyoto thirty years later, in which he drew a connection between his aversion to oral presentation and the core of his theoretical project: it could be, he suggested, that his preference for written language had inspired him 'to draw a distinction of some importance for my theory', the distinction between everyday *communicative action* and *discourse*, the form of communication into which the participants in a conversation switch – according to the theory – whenever they need to subject their problematical claims to a rational validation. The communicative world of Jürgen Habermas is divided into two parts. Our everyday verbal interaction is largely intuitive; only in discourse do those counterfactual presuppositions come into play under which all factors except communicative reason are eliminated. But, inasmuch as our ordinary exchanges are also premised on the possibility of entering into such a clarifying argumentation whenever necessary, the ideal of discourse reveals the normative character of our communicative relations.[6]

This makes the late self-demystification in Habermas's Kyoto speech all the more surprising; he was suggesting that such a concept of discourse could be a projection of his disability. In that case, the distinction between everyday interaction and discourse might stand for the distinction between oral and written communication. The Luhmannian objection that discussions among physically present participants, with their 'terrestrial' shortcomings, bear little resemblance to the exchange of rational arguments with the aim of reaching consensus would then be based on a misunderstanding. In fact, Habermas was not thinking of the endless debates of grassroots leftist groups; what he had in mind was those 'audience-oriented' private citizens scattered throughout the West German provinces, polishing their newspaper articles in the seclusion of their single-family homes – the same ones we encounter as an eighteenth-century ideal in *The Structural Transformation of the Public Sphere*.

In contrast to Habermas's later writings, his predilection for reading and writing is still prominent in that early book. Although the genesis of the bourgeois public sphere is set in the London coffee-houses of the Glorious Revolution, the practice of collective reasoning only becomes a political power as it shifts into the journals and gazettes of the emerging print culture over the course of the century that follows. Just as the responsible individual trains the faculty of reflection through reading and writing, the public sphere of the Enlightenment is by nature a print culture. This is reflected in the negative image produced by that culture's decline. In the last part of his book, Habermas traces the evolution of novel and newspaper readers into irresponsible movie-goers, radio listeners and TV watchers, as a society arises 'which no longer trusts the power of the printed word'.[7]

# Uncanny Germany

Habermas never again put his journalistic activities on hold as thoroughly as he did during his tenure as director of the Starnberg Max Planck Institute. It was a long time since he had felt like participating in public debates, he said in early 1977 to Fritz Raddatz, cultural editor of *Die Zeit*, who had tried to prod him to write.[1] Not until months later, in September, did the philosopher feel called upon to return to the public sphere from the ivory tower of his research institute.

To imagine something of the mood among the West German left in the fall of 1977, you have to watch *Germany in Autumn*, the film anthology about the events surrounding the kidnapping of Hanns Martin Schleyer, president of the German employers' association, and the hijacking of Lufthansa Flight 181. The paranoia with which Rainer Werner Fassbinder wanders – sweaty, chain-smoking and mostly nude – through his nicotine-coloured Munich flat, insulting his lover and flushing his cocaine stash down the toilet because he is afraid of being caught up in a police raid on 'sympathizers', is unforgettable. So is Volker Schlöndorff's footage of the long-haired West German left's procession past the graves of the terrorists Baader, Ensslin and Raspe, the images overlaid with Alexander

Kluge's soft voiceover like a watermark. The same surprise can be felt afresh each time we see Fassbinder arguing with his mother on the telephone about whether one of the terrorists in Stammheim prison should be shot for every hostage killed in Mogadishu, or the German president Walter Scheel invoking the principles of the liberal constitutional democracy at the state memorial service for Schleyer, or the mourners at the terrorists' burial shouting a satirical 'Sieg Heil!' with a stiff-arm salute at the mounted police: almost thirty years after the founding of the West German democracy, hardly anyone seemed to doubt that a relapse into fascism could happen at any moment.[2]

Habermas watched *Germany in Autumn* right after its premiere in the spring of 1978. In his theory of modern society, art has the task of expressing the individual subject and that subject's claim of authenticity. We are relieved to find that his own aesthetic experiences are not restricted to that schematic definition. 'Dear Mr Kluge,' he wrote to his friend of many years after having seen the film, 'without your amazing documentary scenes, without your voice persistently intervening and commenting, without your cuts, always bordering on the malicious, without the Klugean fixation on history and militarism, on fictitious quotations, on incidentals, this film would no doubt have fallen apart and never become something that evokes a tremendous, ambiguous and complex reaction, and inscribes itself permanently in memory.'[3]

Habermas was motivated to speak up not because of the acerbity with which conservative politicians such as Franz Josef Strauss or the future Christian Democrat whip Alfred Dregger condemned the terrorists, but because the right's invective was also directed against the 'verbal radicalism' of intellectuals. Even a liberal political science professor such as Kurt Sontheimer of Munich had summarily declared 'left theory' a breeding ground of political violence. No wonder Habermas felt himself concerned: a categorical boundary needed to be drawn between Starnberg and Stammheim. His various responses to the situation, which he later called one of tension 'like a pogrom', show him at the height of his polemical talent. In *Der Spiegel*, he said the home minister Franz Josef Strauss was trying 'to restore Franco's legacy' in West Germany. Then, in an open letter to Sontheimer, which Heinrich Böll published in his November 1977 anthology of letters in defence of the Republic, Habermas took aim at the 'renegades of the centre'. To those politicians who would stigmatize the use of reason as seditious, terrorism offered a welcome opportunity to declare the left intelligentsia a 'domestic enemy'. The populist resentment being further fanned by the 'deplorable editorials of the *Frankfurter Allgemeine Zeitung*' was, to Habermas, a backlash, a relapse into authoritarian patterns, a slide towards the 'fascistic decay' of the political culture in West Germany. How could Sontheimer, as an 'avowed liberal', allow himself to be drawn into that campaign?[4]

Like the *FAZ* publisher Joachim Fest, like Robert Spaemann, Ernst Nolte and others with whom Habermas had major public disagreements, Sontheimer was a member of his own age group, in whose ranks some of the bitterest political controversies in West German intellectual history have been fought. There were certainly differing ideas among the liberal and democratically-minded forty-fivers about the requirements for a stable German democracy. Habermas later traced this fact to broad differences in experience as a result of small differences in age: 'The unfortunate designation of the "flak-auxiliary generation" obscures the fault line that runs right through the mentalities of this generation. Those who went to war had to risk their necks for Führer and Fatherland, and that brought with it existential experiences, while the exempt cohorts had no such existential baggage to cope with after 1945.' The rebellion of the '68 generation had the effect of a wedge driving the different dispositions apart, polarizing the left-liberal and liberal-conservative intellectuals into opposing camps. In the spring of 1977, Ernst Nolte, a prominent member of the *Bund Freiheit der Wissenschaft* ['Academic freedom alliance'], wrote a letter to Habermas expressing the hope that 'serious university teachers who separated into a "left" and a "right" wing after 1968, under the pressure of events which are difficult to define, could draw closer again today in a new situation'. That hope was premature. In the 'German Autumn' of 1977, the 'civil war' of the forty-fivers reached another high point.[5]

Habermas did agree with the conservatives on one point, however: he never would have denied that West German society was in a severe crisis. Due to the relatively stable economy and social welfare benefits, it was still highly 'integrated' in comparison to Italy or the US, yet the domestic calm seemed to him deceptive. He discerned a disturbing smouldering 'beneath the surface': the growing disenchantment with politics, the increase in 'potential conflicts that are psychologically induced or pushed aside into the private domain' and an 'almost unfathomable fractiousness in social and political interaction', of which terrorism was only the most manifest expression. In his writings from this time, he returns again and again to the oppressed and the offended, the apathetic and the violent, who have fallen through the net of the social fabric. His letter to Sontheimer goes so far as to compare the West German situation with 'that pathological stability that we have seen in studies of sick families'. In 1977, he was farther away than ever from his later satisfaction with West Germany as a total work of art. 'On an intuitive level,' he explained in an interview, 'I'm quite convinced that something in this system is deeply amiss.'[6]

The feeling that Habermas articulates here can also be found in Marie-Luise Scherer's investigations in *Der Spiegel* around that time. Populated by Berlin's junkies, Lower Saxony's full-time campers and other dropouts of the levelled middle-class society, her articles describe a country that consists of discreetly concealed fractures.[7] I can remember the wanted posters with the black-and-white faces of terrorists, and the shivers evoked by Eduard Zimmermann's true-crime TV show *Aktenzeichen XY ... ungelöst* ['Cold case X. Y.'] – and I remember thinking that the local bank in my green Göttingen suburb of Nikolausberg could expect an armed robbery at any time. Alexander Kluge has a catchy phrase for that atmosphere: *Die Unheimlichkeit der Zeit* ['The uncanniness of the time'] is the title of a book of stories he published with Suhrkamp in autumn of 1977 – a labyrinthine tour of the disaster areas of German history that points up disturbing parallels between the Third Reich and West Germany.

In writing stories, Kluge explains in the preface, he deliberately abstains from analysing social conditions. That remark is an allusion to his dual role as a writer and a theorist.[8] But it can also be read as a reference to the division of labour that still connects Kluge today with his alter ego Habermas. They met in the 1950s in the aura of Adorno's mind at the Institute for Social Research. Perhaps it is because of their generation's lucky genes that these two became the unshakable optimists of the Frankfurt School. But since 1962, the year in which Kluge debuted with *Case Histories* [*Lebensläufe*] and Habermas with *The Structural Transformation of the Public Sphere*, the two have divided their inheritance between them over many thousands of pages: while Kluge took on the task of continuing Adorno's convoluted thinking by poetic means, Habermas began refining the prose of theory, purging it of its avant-gardist dross.

# Theory of the Loss of Meaning

Habermas had announced at the outset of the 1970s that he would present his study of language systematically. But not until the crisis of the 'German Autumn' did he feel the necessary urgency to complete his theory of communicative action. His magnum opus is not only a theory of modern society, but also an attempt to wrest the prerogative of interpretation from the conservatives – and that by means of the same critical thinking which they had decried as a danger to the liberal-democratic constitutional order. It is, among other things, a book about the children of the bourgeoisie who had retreated to the 'bastions of dogmatism and alternative lifestyles' instead of getting involved in the democratic institutions. It attempts to identify the fracture at which the uncanny phenomena appeared that caused him concern. 'If one can illuminate somewhat a situation which nobody can really understand, then that has to touch the understanding, even the self-understanding, of broad social groups', Habermas explained to one journalist, underscoring the practical aspiration connected with his theoretical project.[1]

The work that was published four years later, in autumn of 1981, shows little sign of that aspiration. The two volumes, totalling 1,167 pages, tower before the reader like a craggy mountain range. The copy in Berlin's municipal library shows obvious traces of passage of several generations of users. But it also shows that the routes have not all been travelled equally often. A well-beaten track of underlining runs through the 200-page introduction and the chapter on Max Weber's theory of rationalization. The scree slopes of Talcott Parsons's systems theory, on the other hand, are almost pristine. Only in the last chapter, in which Habermas offers a fleeting prospect of the empirical applications of his theory, does the number of pencil marks increase again.

In view of declining sales, Habermas had advised his publisher Siegfried Unseld in the mid-1970s to cut down on the 'political sociology' in the *edition suhrkamp* series, investing more in the 'description of concrete conditions, biographies, case studies' – but, as *The Theory of Communicative Action* demonstrates, he was not about to take his own advice. In vain the reader looks for concrete descriptions or current diagnoses in this work. On the contrary: it has less to say about contemporary society than about the classics of sociology. 'I have written this book for those who have a professional interest in the foundations of social theory', the author says in the preface – and he seems to have been aware of the contradiction with the ambition he had expressed earlier of addressing society at large. Before the publication date, he admitted that his book was 'hopelessly academic' – that he had brought a 'monster' into the world, in fact. Anyone who has ever ventured into that labyrinth of concept clusters, lemmata and contingency tables knows what he meant. It comes as no surprise that it took him several tries to collect the different threads, each of which would have easily filled a Suhrkamp title of its own, under some kind of common rubric.[2]

The 'monster' contains a defence of communicative reason, the analysis of which, Habermas had hoped since the late 1960s, would provide the foundation of his critical social theory.

Proceeding from the norms implicit in our interaction, he undertakes to explain the basis of social order. To that end, he deploys a grand panorama of modern Western society, which he conceives – following the classics of sociology – as the result of layered processes of differentiation. At the beginning is the idea of a form of life which has become steadily more rational, hence more efficient and more productive, but at the same time more just and more humane, by learning to assign different forms of expression, roles, institutions etc. to different aspects of human coexistence. The simple task of ploughing a furrow once involved overlapping religious, political and economic impulses, which have become separated in modern societies. The fault of the classics is just that their conception of this process of separation was too one-dimensional. Habermas's brutally appropriative method consisted in cannibalizing the theories of his predecessors and building their usable parts into a new, dauntingly complex edifice of ideas, which seems to be the destination of a hundred years of European intellectual history.[3]

In the Habermasian version, the process of 'rationalization' begins in the 'lifeworld'. The lifeworld represents the shared horizon of communicative action within which *ego*, in conjunction with *alter*, can take on relations to things, to the other and to the self. Intersubjective communication, which goes on constantly in the lifeworld, then becomes more rational as cognitive, moral and aesthetic considerations separate; that is, as a differentiation arises between questions of knowledge, justice and taste. With time, this leads to an institutionalization of science, morals and art as three cultural 'spheres of value' in which cumulative learning effects give rise to increasingly specialized knowledge and skills. At a certain degree of complexity made possible by this rationalization of the lifeworld, however, a fracture occurs, or rather an 'uncoupling', which lends Habermas's theory its characteristic form: the spheres of value take on a separate existence and coalesce into autonomous 'systems'. Such systems lose touch with the communicative action of the lifeworld, essentially because they switch over from the colloquial language of human communication to specialized languages that are only intelligible to experts – especially in areas concerned not with the symbolic reproduction of society, but with its material reproduction, such as the subsystems of economy and politics. Where the specialized languages – Habermas also calls them 'media' – of power and money rule, the mechanisms of communicative reason are suspended. In modern welfare states, the 'bureaucratic-monetary complex' unfurls its nefarious efficiency not least because it is no longer dependent on the risky venture of mutual understanding.[4]

Habermas's diagnosis of progressive bureaucratization follows the model proposed by Max Weber. With the melancholy of the realist, Weber had accepted that the fate of modern human beings was a life trapped in the 'iron cage' of the systems. In the 'administrated world', according to Adorno, there was nothing else for these human beings to do but to meditate on their powerlessness. Systems theoreticians such as Luhmann and Parsons went so far as to express amazement at the improbable complexity that had evolved in the functional systems of modern society. In Habermas, however, the Marxist legacy breaks through at this point: while Weber emphasizes the inexorable and seamless rationality of the status quo, Marx presents a bourgeois society which – obsessed with the irrational fetish of commodities – is full of explosive internal contradictions. Translating this into the language of sociology, one might say the process of differentiation in this society has not been homogeneously successful. Its astronomical productivity and its smooth efficiency are accompanied by dysfunctional effects, or 'pathologies', that make its crisis inevitable.

At this point, we can return to West Germany in the early 1980s. Having recapitulated a hundred years of the history of social theory and assembled thousands of pieces into a puzzle of monumental dimensions, Habermas boils his theory of communicative action down to a quotable – and often-quoted – aetiology: the crisis of West German society was not the product of the contradiction between the conditions of production and the productive forces, as the Marxists with their obsolete theoretical tools assumed, nor that of modern culture's own decadence, as the neo-conservatives claimed; rather, it was caused by the system's 'colonization of the lifeworld'. Although the Keynesian social welfare state had succeeded in ending class war, the expansion of its bureaucracies was swallowing up all the meaning that the prosperous society could produce: 'Today, economic and administrative imperatives embodied in the media of money and power encroach on areas that somehow collapse when they are disconnected from communication-orientated action and transferred to such interactions steered by these media.'[5]

It was the youth of the middle classes, alienated from their parents, bereft of meaning, who responded to this 'collapse' with seismographic sensitivity. As Alexander Kluge's disturbing documentary footage of autumn 1977 shows, the Daimler-Benz factory halls, where Turkish and Italian migrant workers stood at the assembly lines, were eerily quiet. Only at the terrorists' gravesides was there pandemonium.

# Was That Really Necessary?

In retrospect, it is hard to decide whether *The Theory of Communicative Action* was a triumph or a setback. In autumn of 1981, Siegfried Unseld went to Munich personally to bring Habermas his author's copies fresh off the press – a courtesy that he showed only his especially important authors. The second and third printings were shipped as early as winter of 1981/82, although one reason was that the first print run, at just four thousand copies, had been well below the numbers of Suhrkamp's fat years. 'Long announced, repeatedly postponed and hardly expected any more', the essayist Michael Rutschky noted in his diary about the year's most important new theory publication before he started reading it. The long anticipation alone made the appearance of Habermas's *chef d'œuvre* a cultural event. 'For several months, something has been happening in our country that can only be called a step in our collective learning process', wrote Karl Markus Michel in his review in *Der Spiegel*: 'Almost 10,000 people (and every day there are two dozen more) are bent over a thick book that they cannot ignore.'[1]

There could be no question that the learned author had outdone himself yet again with his new work: the wide range of problems he touched on, the wealth of material he had digested, and the breadth of his systematic ambition were unprecedented. In addition to the theory of communicative action that gave it its title, the book also contained a theory of rationality and a theory of rationalization, a theory of social evolution and a theory of modernity. In spite of this monumental base, its 'clear train of thought' was always visible, the philosopher Rüdiger Bubner stated in his review in *Merkur*. The *FAZ's* critic Jürgen Busche found that Habermas's assimilation of the history of theory developed an 'auratic fascination'. The sociologist Hauke Brunkhorst wrote that Habermas succeeded in showing the way back to Marx 'by moving away from Marx'. But most of the reviewers' praise was followed by reservations – on the whole, the response was disappointing.[2]

To conservatives and liberals, Habermas's conception of an unobstructed communication framework embedded in the lifeworld supplied new evidence of his redemption theology based on faith in language. Quentin Skinner, the founder of the Cambridge School, wrote in a review that dealt lasting damage to Habermas's reception in England: 'Reading Habermas is extraordinarily like reading Luther, except that the latter wrote such wonderful prose . . . We are surely entitled to something more rigorous from our social philosophers than a continuation of Protestantism by other means.' Many on the left would no doubt have agreed, although for different reasons. To the Marxists, the replacement of class struggle by the 'colonization of the lifeworld' amounted to a betrayal of the Marxist legacy; to the adherents of the Frankfurt School, Habermas's defence of modern society expressed a 'disempowerment' of Critical Theory. After having been called a part of the Establishment by the disappointed '68 generation, in the 1980s he was labelled a philosopher in the service of the state.[3]

A strangely emotive, Heideggerian variant of that motif can be seen in the writing of the above-mentioned *FAZ* critic Jürgen Busche. His review starts with the diagnosis of the

West German state's post-tragical character: 'In the country in which hearses only circulate at night, in which old people, up to a certain limit, act young, dynamic, vigorous, only to sink into oblivion once past that limit: in this country, death is repressed.' Observing that the reality of death also goes unmentioned in *The Theory of Communicative Action*, Busche drew the conclusion that the philosopher had capitulated to the West German zeitgeist. Although that logic is strained, to put it cautiously, Busche's critique leads to a sentence that has not lost its pithiness in the intervening years: 'If there is or ever was an experiment called West Germany, then Habermas's philosophy takes an affirmative stance towards it.'[4]

Another new accusation that now made its appearance is that of Eurocentrism. Quentin Skinner, borrowing a phrase from Raymond Geuss, wondered whether Habermas assumed that the universals of communicative reason could also be found among 'pre-dynastic Egyptians, ninth-century French serfs and early-twentieth-century Yanomamö tribesmen'. But apart from the issue of cultural difference, Habermas's theory seemed to neglect the diversity of observable forms of communication among human beings. Much as he might downplay the question and remind the reader that dominance-free discourse is a counterfactual presupposition without which we could not talk to one another meaningfully, was that not in itself a presupposition that reduced communication to mutual understanding, and mutual understanding to consensus? 'Where are wit, humour, irony, cynicism? Where are metaphorical and metonymical speech? Where are fictions and feints – the whole arsenal of good old rhetoric?' asked Karl Markus Michel. Not even Habermas himself would want to live in a world in which communication can only be 'straight' – that is, with claims of truth, correctness and authenticity.[5]

Many critics opined that Habermas's scholastic concept of communication was reflected in the style of his writing. Jürgen Busche reported the impression of having to work through 'evaluations and assessments, reviews and excerpts'. Rüdiger Bubner wrote of 'elements of well-known theories, scientific research programmes and reported approaches' which the author assembled – in a 'selective procedure', moreover – into a collage. Arno Widmann, interviewing Habermas for the *Frankfurter Rundschau,* asked him why he needed 'these constructs, this speaking in different tongues, this terrific willingness to be receptive' in order to articulate his own ideas. The wealth of literature Habermas discussed had long been seen as evidence of his modernity, but now, on the threshold of the 1980s, the image was beginning to form of an unoriginal thinker.[6]

The odd animus that some of us younger students still cultivated in the 1990s, and that was expressed – later still – in Rachel Cusk's fantasy of book destruction mentioned above in 'An Afternoon in Starnberg', is first found, at least in this distinct form, in the responses to *The Theory of Communicative Action.* The text came down on him 'in a kind of snowfall', wrote Michael Rutschky in his journal – a sensation in which he could find a certain 'beauty' only when he stopped fighting it. The Germanist and later novelist Hanns-Josef Ortheil found that was too much to ask. As he confessed in one of the intellectual examinations of conscience that were briefly fashionable then, the 'sentences of the social scientist Habermas' aroused nothing but 'aversion' in him. Karl Markus Michel seems to have had a similar reaction, although he contented himself with a more laconic expression: his review in *Der Spiegel* wickedly concluded with the question: 'Dear Jürgen Habermas: Was that really necessary?'[7]

Urs Jaeggi, reviewing the book for *Die Zeit,* found Habermas's attempt to conceptualize social reality 'old-fashioned, Old-European, insensitive'; Habermas behaved like a 'schoolmaster', prescribing how his contemporaries must think about their discontent in modern society. 'I want to talk about it in my language, and I want to talk about it in the language in which the people interact', Jaeggi wrote. Michel, no stranger to difficult ideas as the mastermind of Suhrkamp's *Theorie* series and an editor of the twenty-volume paperback works of Hegel, went so far as to voice the suspicion that Habermas, with his academic style and his hypertrophic array of concepts, was out to 'humiliate his readers'. It would fall short of the mark to say the reviewer was no longer convinced that the genre of theory merited its authority and its aura as something categorically distinct from common sense. Rather, that distinction had become the main problem: there seemed to be a striking contradiction between the message and the tone of Habermas's critical diagnosis. After all, the reconciliation with decaying modernity that he so vehemently advocated was supposed to depend on the endeavour of enlisting the experts' knowledge to address 'life problems', rather than letting that knowledge go unheard in the corridors of the academies and institutes. But was *The Theory of Communicative Action* applicable to such problems at all? Had it not become disconnected from the lifeworld at the institute in Starnberg? 'Trying to place everyday practice on a systematic, theoretical foundation', Jaeggi asked – 'wouldn't that really suck the marrow out of its bones?'[8]

It is hard to avoid the impression that, with his magnum opus, Habermas pleased none of the people none of the time. While some readers despaired at the unfamiliarity of his language, others found it did not go far enough. Unlike his antagonist Luhmann's sociological concept art, which defamiliarized the most familiar interpersonal situations beyond all recognition, Habermas did not have clear gains to show for his conceptual complexity and high abstraction. The ambition of connecting basic research and contemporary criticism, observers' and participants' points of view, systems and action theory, gave his theory an eclectic nested architecture, but without succeeding at the same time in putting aside the commonplaces of early 1980s cultural criticism. It was no use pointing out over and over again that there was no way of reversing the achievements of modernity, the learning processes that had been kicked off by the differentiation of expert cultures. The dialectics of the loss of meaning in late capitalism that Habermas developed in his book, his critique of the 'system' and its depletion of the lifeworld's 'scarce resources' – and even his mere sketch of an aesthetic theory in which the purpose of art is to permit the subject an authentic expression – looked like a carbon copy of the alternative left's critiques of civilization.[9]

It seems as though Habermas, who up until then had always appeared to be in step with the times, had now missed his cue and, after years of hard conceptual work, released his book into a world that was no longer receptive to its claims of validity. In the year that *The Theory of Communicative Action* appeared, Botho Strauss wrote: 'Without dialectic, we suddenly think dumber, but that's the way it has to be: without it!' Diagnoses of the new political movements and students' disenchantment with theory dominated the West German cultural pages in the early 1980s. In his efforts to assess the situation, Habermas himself kept coming back to the diagnosis of an intellectual climate change. He identified a weariness with everything that had characterized the progressive mind of postwar modernity: abstraction, ambition, confidence in the future, universalism – and of course the 'grand theories'. Instead, there were 'cults of immediacy, the deflation of high standards, anarchy in the soul, celebrations of the concrete on all levels', as he wrote in his introduction to the *Stichworte zur 'Geistigen Situation der Zeit'* [*Observations on 'The Spiritual Situation of the Age'*], the jubilee one thousandth volume of the *edition suhrkamp* series, which he edited in 1979. At Habermas's request, Karl Markus Michel also contributed an article to that anthology. Under the title 'Grundwortschatz des wissenschaftlichen Gesamtarbeiters seit der szientifischen Wende' ['Basic vocabulary of the academic all-round worker since the scientific turn'], he glossed such terms as *Begründungszusammenhang* ['context of justification'], *Herangehensweise* ['approach'] and *Praxisrelevanz* ['practical relevance'] – and under 'S' the lemma *Scheisstheorie*: 'a campus idiom which non-conceptually expresses a justified dissatisfaction with the fundamentally prescientific (metaphysical) arrogance of theories.'[10]

Michel seems to have claimed this aversion for his own in his review of *The Theory of Communicative Action* two years later. At any rate, Habermas counted him among the renegades from that review on – and the fact that he was on the staff of Enzensberger's new culture-cum-lifestyle magazine *TransAtlantik* did not help. 'I am on the most difficult terms with Enzensberger as well as Michel', Habermas wrote in 1982 to the French post-Marxist Cornelius Castoriadis. 'I feel these people are resigned. They alternate between cynicism and conformity.' In accusing both the left and the right of 'neopopulism', he was deploring the sinking intellectual standards visible on all sides. Even Siegfried Unseld expressed his intention to give the 'New Series' of *edition suhrkamp* paperbacks, which began in 1980, a more literary orientation – to Habermas, this seemed a betrayal of the spirit of the previous series. 'You move in a world of Rotary Club members that has nothing in common with me', he wrote to the publisher. At the same time, he resigned as an editorial adviser to the *Theorie* series. He must have written his own *Theory* in full defiance of the darkening times. The comparison with Nietzsche's *Untimely Meditations* suggests itself.[11]

It is symptomatic that the interviewers from *Ästhetik & Kommunikation* were curious to learn what 'libidinous images' fuelled Habermas when he was writing, and where he got his 'moments of happiness ... without which one can hardly understand such effort'. Not only the production of theory, his new readers felt, but also its reception was supposed to bring gratification. The heirs of the New Left could no longer relate to their predecessors' Protestant 'theory work' ethic. To the extent that they were still interested in difficult thinking at all, they were out for quick existential thrills of the kind they obtained from the works of Benjamin or Foucault, or even the cool irony of Luhmann. Roland Barthes had supplied a manifesto of the new hedonism in his essay on *The Pleasure of the Text*, which had been available from Suhrkamp in German translation as *Die Lust am Text* since 1974. Habermas, however, coolly insisted 'that social theory offers no consolation, has no bearing on the individual's need for salvation'. Indeed, he remained quite faithful in this regard to his teacher Adorno: 'A consciousness of the radical absence of consolation is fostered in the first place by theories which inform us about the stages of social development, more mature forms of organization, and the practice through which new social formations can be brought into existence.' His texts had nothing to say to readers who expected profane enlightenment.[12]

The inhabitants of the counterculture and the proponents of experimental lifestyles likewise found nothing to like about the bourgeois Habermas. The editors of the newly founded daily *die tageszeitung* wanted to know whether he too sometimes dreamed of 'packing in' his job as a social theorist and doing 'something else' – a course in alternative medicine, for example. 'The fantasy of doing something like that is a normal part of any midlife crisis, and is found in the inventory of fantasies of any forty- to fifty-year-old intellectual', was his Solomonic answer. Personally, though, he was 'too Protestant by background' to think there was 'progress in happiness'. Nor did he find it plausible that a break with life habits is necessary in order to make new thinking possible: 'You see, if I didn't maintain a fairly old-fashioned, bourgeois form of life, then one necessary condition would be unfulfilled for my being able to think more or less radically, that is to say, without safety precautions and without too much anxiety. The lifestyle of, let us say, the tenured professor or the established author relieves some burdens so that I don't need to worry about the consequences when writing.'[13]

The younger members of the left reacted to Habermas in those days with mutually antagonistic emotions, which attest to their oedipal entanglements with their former role model. Michael Rutschky, for example, imagined overtrumping *The Theory of Communicative Action* with a theory of 'aesthetic-expressive' action that Habermas had not delivered. Rutschky's theory would have given consideration to the bodily aspects of conversation, such as the role played by alcohol and cigarettes, for example. With characteristic ambivalence, Rutschky was still dreaming twenty-five years later of being praised for such a patricide by the father himself: 'A wooden table in a green, summery garden: R. is about to give a speech in homage to Jürgen Habermas, on short notice, off the cuff. Habermas himself comes by, brushes the tabletop with his hand, and gives R. an encouraging nod. R. feels confident and equal to his task, even though he has had no time for any kind of preparation. He will have to rely on his memory. A warm breeze wafts through the garden. R. will concentrate, with swelling expertise, on "aesthetic-expressive action". Habermas has always left it blank, although this is where the greatest challenges await – R. woke up, gratified and unhappily agitated. The idea tormented him again recently that he had failed to attain recognition as "Habermas's younger brother": no commensurate prizes, no opportunities for publication, no platform.'[14]

# Taxonomy of the
# Counter-Enlightenment

For several years it has been a regular exercise in the analysis of contemporary society to date the beginning of the present. The need to establish our position in the flow of time has been a part of the modern identity since the late eighteenth or the early nineteenth century, when the awareness of a dynamic history leading towards an open future first emerged. At that time, Habermas writes in his obituary of Michel Foucault, 'esoteric philosophy' metamorphosed into 'a critique of the present in answer to the provocation of the historical moment'. What is conspicuous about our current diagnosis of the present, in contrast to earlier versions, is that it attempts to decode the essence of the Now by marking its historical beginning. This goes hand in hand with the notion that our Now, Habermas continues, is not simply 'a moment pregnant with decision and bursting under the pressure of anticipated possibilities for the future', but an extended period, a 'broad present', which, fusing vaguely with the future, can only be determined at a distance from its past. Hence the unending succession of 'post-' terms that grace our recent positioning efforts. Our era seems to be meaningful to us only when we conceive it as post-historical, postmodern, postcolonial, post-democratic or postfactual. But each such term begs the question when the given 'post-' began.[1] Is the watershed that defines our political, social and cultural Now the Lehman Brothers bankruptcy, 9/11, or the fall of the Berlin Wall? The various 'histories of the present' that have been published in recent years go back even further. Although they set the accents and the emphasis on different events, they all agree that the sea change occurred at the transition from the 1970s to the 1980s. Some place the critical caesura in the year 1977, some in 1979, some in 1980/81; some see a harbinger of the times that were to come in the broadcast of the television series *Holocaust*, some in the Iranian Revolution, some in the first use of the term 'identity politics'.[2]

These are the years in which Habermas, commuting between Starnberg and various American universities, struggled to complete *The Theory of Communicative Action*. The threshold of the 1980s was also a watershed in his biography. The years preceding this divide seem in many ways like a distant past – one in which we see Habermas on the stage of a darker and at the same time more hopeful West Germany, where mistrust about the Germans' persistently authoritarian dispositions and worries about a retreat from hard-won democratic ground are balanced by broad political horizons and postwar modernity's optimism. Habermas himself once tried to demystify this contrast as an optical illusion: because the political scale of the early West Germany was so heavily weighted to the right, it didn't take much 'to get called a radical'.[3] But that doesn't change the fact that the highbrow Suhrkamp culture, the very idea of founding a Max Planck Institute for a better society, and the belief in the transformative power of theory, for that matter, have long since taken on the Technicolor tones of a retro-futurism in which a weak messianic power seems to slumber on.

Only in the course of the 1980s did a terrain become visible which, in several respects, looks more familiar today. Habermas now conceded more and more often that the situation in

Germany had become 'rather better' – a feeling for which, at the close of the decade, he would invent the term 'fundamental liberalization'. His remark that Rita Süssmuth, the Christian Democrat president of the Bundestag during Helmut Kohl's tenure as chancellor, represented the legacy of '68 proves in hindsight to have been a prophecy of the Angela Merkel era. 'The Long March through the institutions', he stated in 1988 with a certain relief, 'has reached even the CDU.' A few years later, he felt prompted to make his peace with Helmut Kohl himself. Kohl, the unimposing chancellor and provincial European whose initially feared 'spiritual-moral turn' never developed beyond rhetoric, had 'reconciled' Habermas 'with (the old) West Germany'.[4]

That reconciliation was accompanied, however, by a moderation of Habermas's ambitions as a social theorist. In a speech to the Spanish parliament in 1984, two years after Spain's socialists had attained the majority, Habermas admitted a historic defeat: since the 'horizon of the future' had narrowed and emancipation from 'heteronomous labour' had proved unrealistic, it was time to take leave of the utopias of the labour society whose history went back to early socialism. Although he continued to uphold the concept of 'democratic socialism' and exhorted himself in an interview with the *New Left Review* to use it more often again in future, he could only do so because he had separated the term – in a turn that might be called 'post-Marxist' – from the paradigm of labour, and linked it instead to that of communication. That meant his dream of a better society no longer referred to the conditions of production, but to the conditions of communication. 'Socialism will survive', he declared in 1988, 'only if it takes seriously the utopian element that lies within democratic procedures themselves.' After his return to Frankfurt in 1981, Habermas saw the 'reconstruction' of the utopian element – or, more precisely, the normative core of constitutional democracy – as his next major task.[5]

'It is easy to see the beginnings of things, and harder to see the ends', wrote Joan Didion in an essay devoted to her gradual departure from New York. Her sentiment can be easily applied to the era of 'grand theories' which Habermas had embodied for two decades. The years around 1980 are full of unprepossessing events that presage the end of that era. One of them is the provocative 'Praise of Theory' that the philosopher Hans-Georg Gadamer intoned at the meeting of the order Pour le Mérite at the University of Bonn in June 1980. In his ceremonial address, Gadamer pleaded for the revival of an ancient Greek conception of theory that had been forgotten since the days of the student rebellion. Plato and Aristotle, he reminded the assembled members of the order, had meant by *theoria* an attitude of disinterested contemplation, abandoning oneself to observing the world instead of wanting to act on it. 'The old name for theory . . . was admittedly different: philosophy, the love of *sophón*, of true knowledge.' Holding the text of Gadamer's speech side by side with that of Habermas's inaugural lecture from the 1960s, we can see that Gadamer's intention was to revisit precisely that transformation of philosophy into critical social theory which his younger colleague had advocated decades before. While the Greens, in whose ranks many of the New Left began the 'Long March through the institutions', were standing in their first Bundestag elections, Gadamer reclaimed difficult thinking for a conservatism that remained nobly aloof from any aspirations to influence the course of history.[6]

If Habermas had been there to hear Gadamer's poisoned praise at that time – not until some forty years later did the order Pour le Mérite induct him – he would no doubt have interpreted it as another symptom of the 'wave of restoration' which he saw washing over West Germany and putting him on the defensive. The acceptance of the City of Frankfurt's Adorno Prize in September 1980 gave him an opportunity to respond. 'Modernity: An Incomplete Project' was the

title of the acceptance speech that marked the beginning of
the schism – so incisive for my generation – between the
'moderns' and the 'postmoderns'. First, Habermas roughly
sketched the process of social differentiation of science, morals
and art, which he would develop the following year in *The
Theory of Communicative Action*. He underlined, however,
that this process of modernization was not the same thing as
the 'project of modernity' in the title of his remarks, which had
consisted since the French Enlightenment of 'efforts to develop
objective science, universal morality and law, and autonomous
art according to their inner logic' and, at the same time, 'to
release the cognitive potentials of each of these domains from
their esoteric forms' in order 'to utilize this accumulation of
specialized culture for the enrichment of everyday life – that is
to say, for the rational organization of everyday social life'. Like
the concept of the lifeworld, although its thrust is in a different
direction, the project of modernity reflects the endeavour to
regain the unity that has been lost in the rationalized society.
But what Habermas also defined by his 'modernity' was
a standard by which the educated despisers of the modern
could be measured. At the close of his speech, he introduced a
bestiary of 'old conservatives', 'young conservatives' and 'neo-
conservatives', respectively characterized as pre-, anti- and
postmodernists, whose error was that they opposed not only
the dangerous excesses of differentiation, but all attempts to
'release' the potentials of reason accumulated in that process.[7]

The first thing that is remarkable about this taxonomy is
that it dates from the nineteenth and early twentieth centuries.
In this way (and also by his preference for replacing the prefix
'post-' with 'neo-' wherever possible), Habermas implied that
there was nothing new to be expected under the reactionaries'
dark sun. The enemies of modernity, in other words, are rev-
enants, if not throwbacks, of social evolution who can think of
nothing better than to dust off the 'blunted weapons from the
armoury of the Counter-Enlightenment' from time to time.

The philosopher Dieter Henrich, who must have felt himself concerned as a 'neo-metaphysician', described Habermas a few years later as 'ever-resourceful in tracking down conservatisms', and accused him of 'manoeuvring into the desired corner as a harbinger of political philistinism and cultural confusion every change in the theory climate that turned the wind against his interaction paradigm'.[8]

The second thing we stumble over – in surveying the phalanx of his domestic enemies, who include the usual suspects Carl Schmitt and Gottfried Benn as well as the 'neo-conservative' Ritter School and 'old conservatives' such as Robert Spaemann – is the fact that Habermas now adds recent French philosophers 'from Georges Bataille via Michel Foucault to Jacques Derrida'. Representatives of the Counter-Enlightenment abroad – those 'young conservatives' who, inspired by Nietzsche and Heidegger, reacted to the rationality embedded in modernity by celebrating wild subjectivity – 'remove into the sphere of the far-away and the archaic the spontaneous powers of imagination, self-experience and emotion. To instrumental reason they juxtapose in Manichean fashion a principle only accessible through evocation, be it the will to power or sovereignty, Being or the Dionysiac force of the poetical.' In an interview from the same period, Habermas did not hide the fact that he considered 'all this stuff that starts with Bataille' extremely dangerous: 'There are many paths that start from such positions, but most of them lead to perdition when it gets political.' He was at least optimistic enough to think that the worst case was not imminent.[9]

His attack is surprising in that, up to then, he had followed recent French philosophy – with the exception of Existentialism – little more than out of the corner of his eye, and had reciprocated the interest in his work that had resonated from across the Rhine since the 1960s half-heartedly at best. I have mentioned Lucien Goldmann's vain attempts to lure Habermas to France. Habermas's papers also contain a situation report from Paris by the Icelandic sociologist Jóhann Árnason, who informed Habermas in 1971 about a new "'iconoclastic" tendency that extended into the philosophical dimension' and that 'aimed its main thrust at the traditional concept of the subject'. But the all-clear followed immediately: 'The whole problem has come to a dead end, from which the only possible way out is a renewal of dialectical thinking.'[10]

As late as 1974, Habermas had turned down a request from the publisher Axel Matthes for a statement in support of his projected Bataille edition with the explanation that he was not familiar with Bataille's writings. Six years later, this indifference had changed to bitter animosity, and Bataille – along with his poststructuralist disciples – had become a nefarious 'young conservative'. The reasons for this change in his views can be found in the developments within Germany. What put Habermas on high alert was not so much the debate in Paris as its reception in Germany. The new French thought, made available in hasty German compilations by Merve and other small publishers, mesmerized the heirs of the student movement, who were weary of academic Marxism. After years of the strain of communicative learning processes, it must have been an immense relief to read in Foucault – especially in the powerful images of Foucault's prose – that it was time to do away with the categories of language and sign, and instead to analyse social conditions using the model of war and battle. That was one reason why the German versions of terms such as *discours* or *dispositif* took on a subversive aura that they had not brought with them from the French context. The author Lothar Baier opined that the fashion was an artefact of translation. 'French theory', he explained in the early 1980s, was 'Made in Germany.'[11]

By 1978, the *Rowohlt Literaturmagazin* had declared poststructuralism to be the 'new irrationalism'. In the same year, Jean Améry, writing in *Die Zeit*, debunked Foucault as a dangerous Counter-Enlightenment author. Two years later,

Habermas took his place in the line of defence with his apologia of modernity. The fact that Bataille was the first and foremost target of his exorcism draws renewed attention to Bataille's German reception. If Karl Heinz Bohrer, whose study of the 'aesthetics of terror' had contributed to an Ernst Jünger revival, now took a fancy to the theorist of 'expenditure', that placed him in dangerous company. Bataille's most vehement advocate in West Germany was his translator and editor Gerd Bergfleth, whose polemic against the 'jabbering Enlightenment' was aimed not only at Habermas, but also at the 'homeless Jewry' of the older Frankfurt School. Habermas's Adorno Prize acceptance speech was published in a French translation within the year, and Parisians wondered what Bataille and Foucault had to do with a radical conservative current flowing from the Weimar Republic. The French thinkers couldn't know that the gauntlet Habermas was throwing down was aimed at the feet of their German readers.[12]

When the historian Paul Veyne invited him to the Collège de France in 1981, Habermas replied: 'I am extraordinarily glad to have the opportunity for the first time to become more familiar with the intellectual scene in Paris and to cultivate deeper contacts with French colleagues.' The lectures he gave there two years later, in the spring of 1983, form the first part of his book *The Philosophical Discourse of Modernity*. Foucault, who is sure to have read Habermas's taxonomy of conservatisms, did not bother to attend the opening lecture. According to Foucault's biographer Didier Eribon, the dinner with Habermas that he felt obliged to attend a few days later took place in an atmosphere of 'icy politeness'. The two antithetical philosophers had absolutely nothing to say to each other. Habermas, however – perhaps mellowed by age – gives a more favourable account. Instead of an ironical Paris intellectual, he found himself facing a philosopher of impressive 'earnestness'. They talked about their intellectual biographies and discussed New German Cinema. But Habermas too seems to feel a need to mark the limits of their agreement. He favoured Alexander Kluge and Volker Schlöndorff, whereas Foucault – 'naturally' – preferred Werner Herzog, whose jungle drama *Fitzcarraldo* had been released the previous year. In telling the story, Habermas makes it sound as though their different tastes in film revealed the full incompatibility of their philosophical temperaments.[13]

After his return to Frankfurt, Habermas tried to recruit Foucault for an appearance in a new lecture series, the 'Suhrkamp Lectures'. But Foucault had already planned to take a visiting professorship in Berkeley for the autumn, and didn't want to commit to a later date either. According to Eribon, he simply wasn't interested in continuing the dialogue with his German colleague. Although he had discovered the writings of the Frankfurt School just a few years before, and found they anticipated many of his own ideas, various statements from the period indicate that he did not see Habermas as a representative of that style of thinking. While the older Critical Theory had 'disturbed institutional philosophy by shifting the categories towards contemporary political problems', Habermas strove 'to relegate everything that takes place outside the university in the political, cultural and social spheres to an established discourse'. 'I beg you to note', Habermas wrote in his last unsuccessful letter, 'that I am at least making a serious effort to introduce you to the Frankfurt academic community.' In other words, if there was to be no further exchange, it wasn't his fault.[14]

# Distance and *Thymos*

Habermas's feud with the French expresses something that is characteristic of him as a public intellectual in general. For all the universalism with which he argues as a philosopher, he restricts himself as a public intellectual to a particular mission: that of cultivating democracy among his compatriots and helping the norms of universal reason to win through in Germany, the country of the Counter-Enlightenment. To Habermas, even the French young conservatives were a German problem before he met them in person in Paris and delved into their writings. 'At bottom, Habermas has always remained nothing but a theoretician of re-education', his antagonist Peter Sloterdijk once said.[1]

The overlapping of a general concern and a particular one has left its mark in Habermas's work in the form of two different styles of writing. Reading his different texts side by side can even produce the impression of a multiple authorial 'I'. The academic philosopher who prefers to pronounce his unwieldy sentences in 'strange tongues' suddenly transforms into an impulsive thinker who, driven by a 'visible lust for public speaking', deploys a surprising polemical elegance in the melee of debate. Although Habermas's newspaper articles have frequently been collected in books, he has always been clear that his writing on current affairs is only a sideline: 'They obey rules that are less restrictive than those of academic business', he once said about his shorter political essays. A malicious reader might say his division of roles almost amounts to writing from different authorial personas associated with different affective states. The philosopher who coyly claims to be a 'lamentably earnest' thinker assures me he wrote every single one of his newspaper articles out of anger.[2]

Although the polarization of the two authorial roles in his work dates back farther, it was only in the early 1980s that he began to separate them explicitly. It is important, he explained on the publication of the *Theory of Communicative Action*, to 'keep various spheres separate: first of all these political-journalistic things, then "real" philosophizing'.[3] This distinction can be logically derived from his system: all the achievements, all the progress that modernity can be credited with is due in one way or another to processes of differentiation, which is why de-differentiation and mixing – even with regard to academic and public speech – inevitably involves regression, according to Habermas.

That was one reason why he saw the French philosophers as opponents of the Enlightenment. 'Negative dialectics, genealogy and deconstruction alike avoid those categories in accord with which modern knowledge has been differentiated – by no means accidentally – and on the basis of which we today understand texts', he wrote in the *Philosophical Discourse of Modernity*. 'They cannot be unequivocally classified with either philosophy or science, with moral and legal theory, or with literature and art . . . Such discourses unsettle the institutionalized standards of fallibilism; they always allow for a final word, even when the argument is already lost.' In fact, the uncertainty of their genre between social science, philosophy and literature contributed significantly to the fascination of the poststructuralists' books. Texts by Foucault, Derrida, Deleuze

and Guattari seem to have more important tasks to fulfil than
being true. To Habermas, on the other hand, a 'theory' – with
quotation marks to indicate that he thought the label was
undeserved in this usage – that obfuscated its claim to validity
by its genre attribution violated an elementary requirement of
accountability.[4]

The vehemence with which he insisted on distinguishing
between his roles as philosopher and intellectual from the
early 1980s on indicates that his motivation is not merely
theoretical. 'What annoys me terribly,' he explained to his
interviewers, 'what gets to me, is the aggressivity of people
who do not see the role-differentiation in me.' Was he talking
about the often repeated accusation that his political practice
was not consistent with his philosophy? Over the years, Heinz
Bude has not been the only one to notice that the defender
of rational argument does not shrink from sharp judgements
and forceful polemics, and that the theoretician of consensus
tends to divide the world into friends and enemies. If there
was a categorical difference between these separate speech
acts, however – if they went with different kinds of claims to
validity – then they contained no performative contradiction,
his critics' assertions notwithstanding. Habermas's separation
of the spheres followed from his social theory, and was inci-
dentally a dig at the fuzzy language coming from France. At
the same time, however, it can be understood as a strategy to
legitimize his hefty contributions to public debates.[5]

But didn't this distinction, which was so important to him,
amount at the same time to an admission that the unity of
theory and practice that he had insisted on since the 1960s was
a fantasy – in other words, that difficult thinking belonged in
the university while the public sphere was ruled by common
sense? Leftists who clung to 'the belief in the possibility of
introducing theoretical analysis with a middle- or long-range
perspective into day-to-day politics' – to use a phrase of
Habermas's from the 1970s – once more interpreted his ascetic

notion of separate roles as liberal defeatism. 'Just don't muddle things', Urs Jaeggi commented, expressing the suspicion that Habermas as an 'academic pro' no longer wanted to risk subjecting his philosophy to the pressure of the street. What he served his readers instead, Jaeggi wrote, was the 'nouvelle cuisine of theory'.[6]

# J'accuse

In my recollection, the year 1986 is marked by two events: the nuclear meltdown of Chernobyl in April, after which we had to stay indoors when it rained; and the football World Cup in Mexico, the first one I watched on television from beginning to end. I was too young to take note of the fact that, ten days after Germany lost the final to Argentina, Habermas published a newspaper article that has probably been the most influential text of his career.

The *Historikerstreit*, or 'historians' dispute', is one of the watersheds in the West German history of ideas. If we also consider the assessment that it was 'started and won' by Habermas, the picture is one that no Bielefeld School structural history could capture: did an intellectual, acting practically on his own, turn the political culture of a whole country inside out, leaving his mark on it for decades to come? Habermas himself would no doubt reject such a heroizing view. But would he concede that this was his greatest coup? In February of 1986, in a lecture on Heinrich Heine, he had traced the delay with which the French role model of the public intellectual became established in Germany. Only after 1968 had it finally prevailed – and the best indicator that it had was that Germany now had its conservative 'counter-intellectuals' as well. Just a few months later, that hypothesis was put to the test: amid the political obscurity of the 1980s, shortly after the French had solemnly buried the figure of the 'universal intellectual', came the moment of its greatest influence in Germany.[1]

To recapitulate briefly the course of the *Historikerstreit*: in the summer of 1986, the Berlin historian Ernst Nolte argued in an article in the *Frankfurter Allgemeine Zeitung* that the Nazis' massacre of the Jews had been a reaction to the mass murders of Stalinism – that is, an imitation of an originally 'Asiatic deed' – and was thus neither a unique nor an inexplicable event. Shortly before that, Nolte had also maintained, in conversation with the Holocaust survivor Saul Friedländer, that Chaim Weizmann, the president of the World Jewish Congress, had formally declared war on Hitler in 1939, so that the German dictator was justified in treating Jews as enemy soldiers – 'although not in killing them, of course'.[2]

However, in contrast to what is written in some retrospective summaries today, Nolte's article did not provoke any 'storm of indignation' at the time. Only the publication of Habermas's response in *Die Zeit* a month later made a political issue of Nolte's theses, the principles of which had been advanced as early as 1963 in Nolte's textbook *Three Faces of Fascism* [*Der Faschismus in seiner Epoche*]. Habermas rejected the comparison and the chain of causation between Auschwitz and the Gulag as whitewashing apologetics. More grave, however, was his identification of Nolte's article as part of a campaign by revisionist 'NATO historians' who, as agents of the current chancellor's historical policy, were pursuing a 'revival' of the battered German national consciousness. Just the previous year, on the fortieth anniversary of the unconditional surrender, Helmut Kohl had staged a symbolic reconciliation with the American president Ronald Reagan at the military cemetery of Bitburg. Habermas cited the singular crimes against humanity of the Holocaust as a veto against such attempts to 'normalize' Germany's past: 'Because of that horrible break in continuity, the Germans have given up the possibility of constituting their political identity on something other than universalist principles of state citizenship, in the light of which national traditions can no longer remain unexamined, but can only be critically and self-critically appropriated.' Moreover, he noted, opinion surveys showed that the citizens of the Federal Republic were in fact tending towards such a 'constitutional patriotism'. A distant echo of Hegel's 'cunning of reason' can be heard in Habermas's satisfaction 'that we have not completely wasted the opportunity that the moral catastrophe could also represent'.[3]

The ensuing dispute, which quickly grew heated, played out on several levels: politically, it concerned the treatment of the history of the Nazi period; academically, the issue was Holocaust research. In the mid-1980s, it was by no means decided, as the Kohl government's statements on history made clear, whether the Germans had been 'defeated' in 1945 or 'liberated'; nor whether, after forty years, it was time to wrap up the historical appraisal of Auschwitz or to start it in earnest. We can hardly believe our eyes when we read today that Raul Hilberg's pioneering study *The Destruction of the European Jews* had been translated into the language of the perpetrators only four years earlier – two decades after its original American publication – by an alternative publisher in West Berlin. By the mid-1980s, German historians had not published a single comprehensive study on the subject. Up to then, research had focused on other aspects of Nazism, such as the *Machtergreifung*, the power structure of the regime, or the conduct of the war. But left-wing theories of fascism too, in deriving the crimes of the Hitler regime from its capitalist nature, had demoted the murder of the Jews to a 'secondary contradiction'.[4]

The clarity with which the debate brought to light the historians' omissions does not explain the uproar that it caused.

The historian Ulrich Herbert has called it a 'proxy war between West Germany's political camps'. As almost all the participants' ages indicate, what began in 1986 was the last battle of the 1945 generation's long war for the mentality of the German postwar democracy. Was it fitting, after forty years, to let the past finally be past, and find a way back to a positive identity, or was the remembrance of Auschwitz the only thing that could prevent a relapse into authoritarian patterns – hence a kind of 'negative national interest'? As the 1980s came to a close, it was already undisputed in the West German public sphere that the left-liberal camp associated with Habermas had won the dispute. While Ernst Nolte, who seems to have been completely insensitive to the subtle differences between academic and public debate, talked himself into increasing disfavour on television, a broad consensus gained the upper hand which held that the Holocaust could neither be relativized nor 'laid to rest' – not within the limits of legitimate political discourse. In 1988, Habermas 'breathe[d] a little more easily' that there were now 'majorities in Germany that we don't have to be afraid of'. And although he may well have doubted that estimation again since, he underscored it twenty years later when he declared that the *Historikerstreit* had 'planted stakes on the field of memory politics that would no longer be moved by the political elites in Germany'.[5]

Another sixteen years later, the situation is different: on the one hand, there are once again nationalist politicians shaking the boundary markers of the commemorative culture that became established in Germany through the *Historikerstreit* – and through the subsequent debate on the project of a memorial to Europe's murdered Jews in Berlin; on the other hand, the question has also been raised whether that commemorative culture is starting to become a paralytic liturgy. In 2021, the Australian historian Dirk Moses (mentioned above in 'Perpetrators and Victims') triggered the 'Second *Historikerstreit*' with his polemic against the 'Germans' catechism'. To Moses, and

to other participants in the debate, it was mainly the pos-
tulate of the singularity of the Holocaust that had changed
from an instructive, discourse-broadening thesis into a dog-
matic pronouncement. Singularity was now being asserted,
they observed, for the purposes of discrediting comparative
research on the relation between the murder of the Jews and
crimes of colonialism, and of preventing a 'responsible' public
discussion about Israel. As early as 2015, the Israeli philosopher Omri Boehm had criticized Habermas's refusal to address
the Netanyahu government's settlement policy as a breach of
the universalist principles that he had devoted his work to
establishing: 'A German who refuses to comment on Israel's
behaviour refuses to take the position of the Enlightenment
when it comes to Jewish affairs.'[6]

The Hamas terror attack of 7 October 2023 and the war
in Gaza have made this debate unexpectedly controversial.
In November 2023, as I write this chapter, Habermas has
harshly condemned the new outbreak of anti-Semitism in a
joint statement with colleagues at the University of Frankfurt.
He reminds us that 'Jewish life and Israel's right to exist' are
'central elements which merit special protection' in Germany
because of the crimes of the Nazi state. Furthermore, 'those
in our country who have cultivated anti-Semitic feelings and
beliefs under all kinds of pretences' have no right to take Israel's
legitimate military defence as an excuse to give free rein to such
feelings – this passage apparently referring mainly to Muslim
immigrants. The condemnation of anti-Semitism in all its vari-
ants is a necessary signal. However, the fact that Habermas and
his co-authors say not a word about the complexity of the
political situation in the Middle East, nor about Islamophobia
in Germany, which is also feeding on recent events, indicates
that their universalism runs up against a limit here which is
rooted in the moral economy of pre-unification West Germany.
If, as they write, the 'elementary rights to freedom and physical
integrity as well as to protection from racist defamation' are

to apply equally to all, then why do they overlook the defamation of the other side, regardless of their legitimate support for Israel? This leads back to what Habermas had regarded as the critical question during the *Historikerstreit*, arising in a new way today: is a commemorative culture based on the affirmation of the singularity of the Holocaust still appropriate to cultivate a universalist, republican attitude in the minds and hearts of all Germany's inhabitants?[7]

It is remarkable that the German Jewish philosopher Ernst Tugendhat, whom Habermas had brought to Starnberg for a period in the 1970s, formulated a critique of the singularity thesis as early as July 1986 which anticipated the current debate in several respects. 'Please don't misunderstand me', he wrote to his friend the day after his polemic had appeared in *Die Zeit*. 'I think that Auschwitz is, for both Germans and Jews, a unique historical trauma that no one can ignore. For us it is unique, but the lessons we should learn from it, Germans and Jews, should be universal. We must turn the sensitivity that has arisen from our lot into a universalist sensitivity – we must, otherwise we are stuck in the vicious circle of particularism. Thus unique events can be inducements, but not arguments. Both the Jews and the Germans tend to feel themselves unique, and hence to see their part – positive or negative – as unique. That can only lead to the facts being fenced in, and events that are in fact comparable being understated, both in Israel and here.'[8]

It would be interesting to know what Habermas answered at the time, but there is no reply to Tugendhat in his papers. Perhaps he insisted, with reference to Hegelian dialectics, that the universal norms of reason, which always require a historical embodiment, can only be effective in Germany through the acknowledgement of an extreme particularity. In the reaction to Dirk Moses that Habermas published in 2021, while conceding that 'all historical facts can be compared with other facts', he insisted that the Nazis' intention had not been to exploit a

colonized population, but to 'extinguish without exception' a
'domestic enemy' – a difference exposed by the comparison, no
matter what significance one might attribute to it.[9] However,
it is important to recall with regard to the debate Habermas
provoked in 1986 that the prohibition of comparisons with the
Holocaust was neither an epistemological nor a metaphysical
position, but a political one, which, in the context of the time,
took on a kind of strategic singularity itself. To do justice to
Habermas's role – and his coup – in the *Historikerstreit*, we
must recapitulate it in reverse chronological order.

In contrast to the ancient Roman strategy of *divide et impera*,
he practised the art of conquering his foes by amalgamation.
Not only did he characterize four very different historians
as a shock troop of revisionism – Michael Stürmer, Andreas
Hillgruber, Klaus Hildebrand and Ernst Nolte – but he also
succeeded in winning the diverse fronts which 'modernity'
had been defending for years against the 'restoration' by con-
centrating them all into one arena: the treatment of the Nazi
period. In the *Historikerstreit*, he continued his fight against an
abridged, 'neo-conservative' conception of modernity, against
the 'neo-populism' of the 'new tendency', and against the intellectual slackening after '68 – but with the crucial innovation of
taking the fight into the history departments.

The ideological fronts between historians had become more
permeable after the debates of the 1960s and '70s, but now
the field very quickly fell apart, as if by electrolysis, into two
opposing camps. Habermas's papers contain whole bundles of
letters from historians who wrote to him to communicate their
approval. Wolfgang Mommsen was 'very much taken' with his
intervention. Hans-Ulrich Wehler, who had advised Habermas
on his reply to Nolte, developed the battle plan for the left-
liberal camp. Martin Broszat too, the director of the Institute
for Contemporary History in Munich who had chimed in with
an approving commentary in *Die Zeit*, assured Habermas of
his support. He was interested, he wrote, in 'presenting the

merit of your intervention and the fabulous inspiration that guided you in publishing it in the proper light against the Habermasophobia that can be observed even among the left members of our discipline when it comes to publicity'.[10]

The members of the other camp expressed outrage at being ideologically patronized. Because the attack was led by an outsider, they also felt their field was being instrumentalized, if not abused. Klaus Hildebrand found that Habermas had a 'dysfunctional relationship' to historical research; Thomas Nipperdey, one of the few who tried to de-escalate the conflict, said the debate was a 'misfortune' for the discipline; Imanuel Geiss, who had been involved in the controversy over Fritz Fischer's claims in the 1960s, saw the delegitimization of conservative historians as a danger to democracy. Habermas's rejection of such accusations as 'ruffled feathers about the confounding of politics and scholarship' says a great deal about the tone of the debate. Perhaps in part because of fundamental reservations against the discipline – about which we will have more to say anon – he seems to have responded with a certain indifference to the genuine cognitive interests of historians. In any case, although he was otherwise scrupulously attentive to distinctions of genre and speaker's role, he had no qualms about dedifferentiation in his dispute with the historians.[11]

More important than his style, however, is the fact that he entered the political arena of history at all. To say that Habermas was victorious in 1986 is only half the story. His victory came at the price of accepting his 'neo-conservative' opponents' choice of weapons: as he had repeatedly established in his topical essays since the early 1980s, they were reacting to the crisis of West German society with symbolic sidestepping, and one such manoeuvre was the attempt to brand the intellectuals as domestic enemies. 'On the other hand, traditional culture and the stabilizing forces of conventional morality, patriotism, of bourgeois religion and folk culture are to be cultivated.'[12]

Habermas had tried to redefine the terms of the debate with
*The Theory of Communicative Action* by taking the analysis to a
deeper level. But only during the course of the *Historikerstreit*
did he too begin to argue in cultural rather than social categories, and to substitute – as his opponents did – metapolitics, the
struggle for hegemony, for the practice of theory. It is revealing
that, in referring to the concept of 'constitutional patriotism', he
adopted an attitude that had until then been taboo among the
West German left. At the same time, he continued to criticize
the 'new intimacy between culture and politics', because 'once
a person communicates in terms of culture, they can persuade
only in the dangerous medium of beliefs'. Thus he should have
agreed with the philosopher Christoph Türcke, who in late
1986 was indignant that none of the parties to the debate mentioned capitalism. In that vein, the historian Ulrich Herbert
wrote, summing up the consequences of the *Historikerstreit*:
'The front was no longer defined by the contradiction between
capital and labour, by the demand for "more democracy" or for
détente and *Ostpolitik*. The categories of left and right are now
determined mainly by relations to Nazi history.'[13]

Thus we might say that Habermas himself contributed to
the very 'neo-historicism' that he identified as a part of the
conservative backslide. The impression I described above of
having crossed the threshold to the present day in Habermas's
footsteps sometime in the 1980s has to do with a very literal
turning point in time – the moment when he turned away
from modernity's broad horizon to face instead a past that held
unbroken dominance over the 'unredeemed present'.[14]

# Back from the Future

In a way, history was of course evident in Habermas's work from the beginning. His insistence on the possibility of a more humane society was a response to the cataclysmic experiences of 1945. In 1953, he accused Heidegger of wanting to legitimize 'the planned murder of millions of people' in terms of his philosophy of Being. In his 1966 review of Karl Jaspers's alarmed appraisal *The Future of Germany*, he concurred with the author's critique of the 'let's-move-on mentality' of the political class. The Bundestag's resolution to extend the statute of limitations for 'crimes of Nazi terror' for only four more years, but not to repeal it outright, was yet another confirmation 'that we do not want to assume political liability for that state which was once borne up by rejoicing masses and backed by prominent individuals'. Two years later, in *Knowledge and Human Interests*, Habermas developed the idea that the society as a whole could reassimilate its 'lost life history', and although the connection was not explicit, we can understand that idea as an attempt to come to grips with this refusal of responsibility by other than legalistic means. After all, in Frankfurt he had come under the influence of a philosophy for which Auschwitz formed an ineluctable point of reference. But didn't his gradual emancipation from Adorno's negative dialectics also require a liberation from this paralysing orientation? It is conspicuous in any case that, in the 1970s, a decade the historian Norbert Frei has called 'peculiarly ahistorical', the Holocaust practically disappeared from Habermas's work.[1]

If the 'belated modernization' of the young West Germany was based on looking forward and not back, the same can be said, with significant qualification, of Habermas. Nietzsche postulated in his text *On the Advantage and Disadvantage of History for Life* the incompatibility of forward-looking action and backward-looking memory: the power to act, he found, is dependent on the ability to forget. In 1983, Hermann Lübbe's concept of 'communicative silence' expressed an analogous idea with regard to the functional requirements of German postwar society. Not only the period of economic and political reconstruction offers a wealth of examples for his thesis; so too does the mental reconstruction. In spite of its drive to denounce the sins of the fathers, the '68 movement was also characterized by an 'avoidance of concreteness'. The 'summer of theory' was a lean time for history.[2]

Now that the humanities and cultural studies have long since set off down the royal road of historicism, it is hard to imagine the marginalized position to which history was relegated during the 1960s. In his closing talk at the 1970 *Historikertag*, the biannual conference of the German Association of Historians, Reinhart Koselleck summed up the social, political and epistemological devaluation that his discipline had suffered since 1945. Unable by definition to fulfil demands to 'manage' the past, history had at the same time declined in epistemological status through the rise of the social sciences. With the business of writing history so endangered, Koselleck advocated remedying its 'need for theory' by accelerated theorization. His colleague Wolfgang Mommsen was thinking in a similar direction, although he had a different kind of theory in mind. In the inaugural lecture he had given in Düsseldorf in 1970,

Mommsen advocated a social science of history 'beyond historicism', which would help, as a 'true partner of the other social sciences', to give 'the present a greater degree of rational orientation'.[3]

The diction itself brings us closer to the notions of a future history that Habermas harboured at that time – except that Habermas, less optimistic than Mommsen and Koselleck, drew a categorical boundary between the language games of 'theory' and 'narrative'. While he did not challenge history's *raison d'être*, he did emphasize that history, a narrative form of knowledge, was 'not theoretical' – that is, it was only capable of statements about past events. For lack of a clear division of the interpretative domains, he refused even to concede a higher status to the knowledge of historians than to the general 'historical awareness of contemporaries'. Adopting sociological terms, as his schoolmate Wehler did in Bielefeld, seemed insufficient to Habermas to release history from its 'narrative reference system'. Looking at his preliminary studies from the 1970s on the differentiation of modern society, we get the impression that he hoped someday to surmount the writing of history by means of a theory of evolution underlaid with historical research, which – far from being limited to reconstructing the past – would infer future developments from the 'structural possibilities' of the present.[4]

Habermas had related ideas at that time about national identity and collective memory. On receiving the city of Stuttgart's Hegel Prize in 1974, he devoted a whole acceptance speech to the topic. The basic ideas were visibly borrowed from the new social theory of communication that he had just begun working on. He began by explaining that modern society is still dependent for its cohesion on a collective feeling of belonging – Luhmann notwithstanding, who wanted to relegate human beings and their need for meaning to the environment of social systems. However, Habermas continued, that feeling of belonging can no longer be fostered in the customary way – that is, by reference to cultural tradition, national community or a certain territory. Even the 'sovereign constitutional state' that Hegel had once invoked was no longer apt as an anchor point for 'rational identity', Habermas found, because of persisting class structures and economic globalization. Instead, he sketched the possibility of a 'post-conventional' universalist identity that would arise from the consciousness of belonging to a community of communication in which the shared values are subject to debate: 'A new collective identity, if it ever comes into being . . . would be an identity non-prejudiced in its content and independent of particular organizational types, of the community of those who engage in the discursive and experimental formation of an identity-related knowledge on the basis of a critical appropriation of tradition as well as of the inputs from science, philosophy and the arts.' Note that the whole description is in the conditional mood. Habermas was not so naive as to assume that such a post-national, post-territorial, post-state society had already been achieved somewhere. In keeping with his universalist conception, he built his argument without recourse to cultural or historical idiosyncrasies. Nonetheless, it is remarkable to hear him say in passing that 'things that were culturally taken for granted have been worn out and the traditional claims to validity have been undermined'. The real name of the experiment in identity politics that Habermas was advocating is West Germany.[5]

If only it hadn't been for 'neo-historicism'! Just when theory seemed ready to supplant history, and the network of communication about to replace national identity, Habermas couldn't help observing a conservative backlash here too. The intellectual deficiencies, the syndrome of 'neo-conservatism', 'neo-populism', 'neo-Aristotelianism' and all the other revisionisms that he had noted with growing concern since the mid-1970s, also involved the return of the past. As postwar modernism's promise of progress eroded, backward-looking passions came to light. They were revealed in the form of a sudden popularity of historical exhibitions and museums, retro cycles in pop culture, and hobby historians and armchair genealogists combing the archives and attics in search of local, family and everyday histories. As the sheen of theory faded, history became attractive to the left too: the History Workshops that came into being in many West German cities in those days were an offshoot of the alternative movement. In 1987, the critic Gustav Seibt observed an 'almost violent return of the historical in the West German consciousness'. After Wolfgang Mommsen had diagnosed an atrophied sense of history in fast-moving modern society at the outset of the 1970s – the reason why the task of preserving the collective memory was entrusted to professional historians – many of his colleagues complained towards the end of that decade not of atrophy, but of inflation and trivialization.[6]

Habermas's primary concern, meanwhile, was the political implications of that neo-historicism. In 1974, Golo Mann, whose biography of Wallenstein was a best-seller that year, had advocated a return to picturesque historical narrative. 'There is a time for theory and a time for practice . . . if I read the signs correctly, the desire to get back to the subject itself will win out', was his patronizing prediction. The historian Thomas Nipperdey of the University of Munich earned academic stature with a similar position, and in the 1990s we read his three-volume German history of the nineteenth century as an epic alternative to Hans-Ulrich Wehler and the Bielefeld School. Habermas would have been less worried if he had seen the divergence merely as a methodological dispute among historians. But the goal the critics of historical social science were really pursuing, in his view, was to open their guild once more to conventional narratives of national identity and to foster a sense of historical continuities by means of empathy for past perspectives and moods. This tendency reached its alarming climax in the 1980s with Andreas Hillgruber's and Ernst Nolte's willingness to empathize even with Hitler.[7]

To make matters worse, progressives too felt the new need for historical identity – progressives such as the director Hans-Jürgen Syberberg, who indulged his fascination with Nazism in his 1977 *Hitler: A Film from Germany*; or the Frankfurt *Sponti* Thomas Schmid, who publicly declared that he 'no longer wanted to cover up' his Germanness; or Karl Heinz Bohrer, who in 1979 in the *Frankfurter Allgemeine Zeitung* advocated engaging again with Germany 'as an intellectual option', in opposition to the inoffensive social democratic conception of culture. But it may have bothered Habermas much more that the self-declared communist Martin Walser, who had protested alongside him during the 'German Autumn' of 1977 against the defamation of left-wing intellectuals, was now making German nationalist noises.[8]

After becoming acquainted in the Suhrkamp circle of the 1960s, Habermas and Walser had developed a family friendship over the course of the subsequent decade, in part because their children were the same age; they exchanged visits in Starnberg and Nussdorf, took their families on holidays together, met up during concurrent sojourns in the United States. Habermas became an important point of reference for Walser, whose journals reveal a growing insecurity about his status as an author (although he had just achieved one of his greatest successes with the novella *Runaway Horse*). 'Except for Jürgen Habermas, I find no one entirely tolerable any more', he noted in 1977. In a dream, they fly through the night sky, holding each other tight – as if Habermas were the only one who could save him from the fall he feared. The offence Habermas gave by questioning their friendship in June 1979, at his own fiftieth birthday party, was all the greater. Walser must have given him his contribution to the *Observations on the Spiritual Situation of the Age* shortly before, as the book had been announced for Suhrkamp's autumn catalogue. In his essay, titled 'Handshake with Ghosts', Walser had finally expressed an inner unrest: in defiance of the left-liberal main stream, which he said 'rejects history', he confessed his need to 'overcome historically the condition known as West Germany', and then to find the way back to a national identity 'that might be called natural'.[9]

At his birthday party, Habermas, never at a loss for a trenchant opinion, gave Walser to understand what he thought of such needs. In Walser's presence, he explained to the literary critic Peter Hamm that Walser had written 'a bad and terribly nationalistic essay'. Walser's journal entry continues: 'Before that he had called out vinously to a larger circle that I was, chronologically, his last friend, the very bottom of the list, and he had to consider whether he shouldn't draw a line there.' Was the ire that boiled up in Habermas the same one that drives him – then as now – to make his political statements? However that may be, Walser took offence. He left the party to go home long before midnight with the bitter feeling that he had been humiliated.[10]

But Walser's hurt pride was not only on Habermas's account. The guests had also included Siegfried Unseld, whose very slightly distant behaviour Walser thought he could read as a decline in his literary valuation. But it was most of all Gershom Scholem, Walser's journal discloses, who spoiled his evening. Scholem, who came to Germany regularly in those days, and on such occasions usually stopped in Starnberg, was the focus of the party. 'Gershom Scholem can be seen always going on at someone with windmill arms . . . When Siegfried or Jürgen Habermas introduces guests to him or drags them over to him to say hello, he doesn't recognize them, even if they tell him they met him in such and such a place the day before yesterday or a month ago. And anyway what he wants is to go on talking.' Walser, accustomed to being the centre of attention himself, felt he had been socially demoted to a minor character. His attempt to get a word in edgewise had ended disgracefully because he hadn't known that blue and white were the colours of the Zionist movement in 1920s Berlin. Scholem's description of such slow wits as 'goyish fogginess' did nothing to improve Walser's mood. 'Marcuse is constantly amazed at Scholem's memory and knowledge. About Bloch and Rosenstock-Huessy, for example . . . "He was from Breslau", I say, just to say something. Gershom Scholem: "And how!" And gets yet another laugh.' And Scholem drank only orange juice the whole evening, while Walser couldn't bring off a *bon mot* even after several glasses of wine. He suddenly felt too old for the gold chain he had borrowed from his wife for the evening. 'I buttoned my shirt collar. We were already leaving anyway.'[11]

More than forty years ago, in the same sofa corner in which Habermas extends his trainers towards me today, the trenches of what we call *Vergangenheitsbewältigung*, coming to terms with the past, were thus dug: Walser, who would later call for an end to German guilt in his speech in the Frankfurt Paulskirche, was already persuaded in the 1970s that his compatriots should return to a national identity 'that might be called natural', and felt his vanity offended by one of the influential figures of German commemorative culture. 'Only in remembering the past,' Scholem had said before the 1966 World Jewish Congress in Brussels, 'only in remembering the past, the meaning of which our minds will never fully be able to perceive, can there grow a new hope for the reestablishment of the dialogue between Germans and Jews – for the reconciliation of those who are today separated'. That was the position Habermas later maintained in the historians' dispute. Walser, on the other hand, saw the 'unceasing presentation' of Auschwitz as an 'exploiting of our disgrace'.[12]

Habermas accepted Walser's 'terribly nationalistic' essay – which prefigures important motifs of his 1998 speech in the Paulskirche – for his compendium of the Suhrkamp culture: it appears prominently as the first chapter in *Stichworte zur 'geistigen Situation der Zeit'* (although it is not included in the English translation of that book, *Observations on the 'Spiritual Situation of the Age'*). That too is an indication of how the fronts have shifted since then: in 1979 their friendship only suffered a thin crack; not for another twenty years would it end in a falling-out. Nor would the murmurings of nationalism that were heard among West German intellectuals have condensed, in Habermas's view, into a chain of evidence of neo-conservative historical revisionism if it hadn't been for the change of government in 1982. Soon after taking office, Chancellor Kohl announced his plans to open two museums of German history as a part of his 'new spiritual and moral direction'. At the same time, with his doctoral degree in history, he took over the direction of the commemorative calendar: 1983 would mark the fiftieth anniversary of Hitler's seizure of power, 1984 the fortieth anniversary of the 20 July plot, and 1985 the fortieth anniversary of the end of the war. The handshake between generals Ridgway and Steinhoff in the presence of Kohl and Reagan in Bitburg, which Ralf Dahrendorf called the 'most symbolic public event' of that time, was intended as a gesture of reconciliation with great publicity value. That plan was thwarted by the fact that the cemetery contained not only the graves of German and American soldiers, but also those of Waffen-SS members. Fortunately for Kohl, three days later the West German president Richard von Weizsäcker managed to restore the country's good reputation with its Western allies with his famous speech in which he declared the Allies' victory a 'liberation' and called for the erection of 'a memorial of thought and feeling inside us'.[13]

The Bitburg controversy, raised even before Reagan's visit especially by American Jews – Elie Wiesel called the planned visit a 'vindication of the SS' – was the occasion for Habermas's first commentary on the new politics of history. Kohl's attitude towards the German past, Habermas wrote, in a metaphor typical of the time, was like that towards 'a nuclear power station for whose radioactive waste no permanent disposal site has been found.' When the German Publishers' Association and the city of Munich awarded Habermas the Scholl Siblings Prize in 1985 for his essay collection *Die neue Unübersichtlichkeit*

['The new obscurity'], he took the occasion to reflect on the
legacy of Sophie and Hans Scholl, the young anti-Nazi activists
of the White Rose underground organization. In his acceptance speech, Habermas alluded to an inverse temporal effect
that observers from all political camps were experiencing in
the West Germany of the mid-1980s: with increasing historical distance, the burden of the 'nightmarishly recurring past'
seemed not to diminish, but to increase. 'It is as if those twelve
years were growing under the pressure of constant renewal,
instead of shrinking as the perspective becomes ever more
remote.'[14]

# History and Memory

In fact, there was suddenly no escape from the darkest chapter of German history. A week after his speech, Habermas received an invitation to a colloquium on 'collective processes of commemoration in relation to the Nazi period', organized by Saul Friedländer, a fellow at the newly founded *Wissenschaftskolleg*, or Institute for Advanced Study, in West Berlin's Grunewald Forest in February 1986. Was he being invited because of his most recent statement, his role as the head of the Frankfurt School, or his friendship with Gershom Scholem? In addition to Habermas and his wife, Friedländer was able to bring an impressive line-up to Berlin, including leading German historians such as Hans Mommsen, Heinrich August Winkler and Lutz Niethammer; German Jewish intellectuals such as Dan Diner, Micha Brumlik and Marianne Awerbuch; and a diversity of experts, among them the Göttingen psychiatrist Joachim-Ernst Meyer, the Israeli historian of philosophy Amos Funkenstein, and the American sociologist Norman Birnbaum. The intelligentsia of West Berlin was represented by the philosopher Margherita von Brentano, Jacob Taubes and Nicolaus Sombart – to name only the most renowned participants. It is a shame that Reinhart Koselleck was in

New York and Christa Wolf was denied an exit visa to visit from East Germany: it would have been exciting to see the course the debate would have taken if the liberal-conservative and the East German author had been able to accept the invitation. Friedländer's colloquium was met with great interest. As he later recalled, every seat in the lecture hall of the *Wissenschaftskolleg* was filled.[1]

There had never been an event like this one in Germany before. The first academic conference on the Holocaust in West Germany had been held just two years before, in 1984 in Stuttgart, and had dealt with the 'resolution and realization' of the genocide in the Nazi regime. Friedländer, who had participated in the Stuttgart conference along with Mommsen, now shifted the focus from the crime itself to its social aftermath – in the US, in Israel and especially in West Germany. The phenomena of collective memory and the latency of trauma, subjects of inflationary discussion today, had only just appeared on the horizon of research at that time. Besides the academic issue, Friedländer was apparently interested in instigating a German–Jewish dialogue, and that in precisely the place where Gershom Scholem, long the most prominent critic of such an endeavour, had been a fellow in the winter of 1981/82, shortly before his death.[2]

The conference was taped, and the transcript, which is preserved in the library of the *Wissenschaftskolleg*, is an unusual document. It does not reflect the objective tone of critical distance which is characteristic of such gatherings. Neither the German nor the Jewish scholars were able to approach the topic purely academically, it appears, but instead kept reverting to the role of eyewitnesses. 'The appeal, and certainly the burden too, of this conference', remarked Peter Wapnewski, the rector of the *Wissenschaftskolleg*, at some point during the two-day event, 'consists of course in the personal involvement of every participant, which is quite unlike speaking about a historically remote subject.' In his closing statement, Friedländer went so far as to conclude that, without the 'emotional individual digressions', the conference would have failed to achieve its purpose.[3]

The degree of consternation among the participants was in keeping with the controversial character of the discussion. There was unanimity only with regard to the perceived common enemy, the neo-conservative historical revisionists from the 'bourgeois bloc'. As the transcripts indicate, all the other issues concerning the Holocaust and its aftermath discussed on both days remained undecided. What was the relationship between history and remembrance? In addition to the Jewish survivors, weren't the German perpetrators also traumatized? Was Auschwitz a singular event? Did that event have a supra-historical dimension? Had it long since become the de facto 'central symbol' of the Nazi regime? Was remembrance generally dependent on symbols and monuments, or did such symbolic expressions – in Israel, in West Germany – necessarily turn into nationalism? What to make of many West Germans' fascination with Israel, or the 'pluralization of the Holocaust' by American minorities? Did the burden of history prevent the Germans from forming a constructive policy on the Middle East? Should the Germans' efforts so far to analyse and evaluate the past be seen as successful first steps, or as failure?

Most importantly, however, there was no consensus on what one participant called the crucial question: had the psychological repression begun only after the end of the Third Reich, or while it still ruled? What had the Germans known about the massacre of the Jews before 1945? Hans Mommsen, born in 1930, made little impression with his reference to the existing research on this question – the urge to bear witness was stronger, especially among the older participants. When Margherita von Brentano, born in 1922, insisted on the second day 'that every person over 15 in this country at least could have known, and actually did know', Peter Wapnewski, two days older than her, who had only listened up to then, could not stay in his seat. As a private in the tank corps on the eastern front, he had 'never heard even a hint about what is being described here as the terrible fate of the Jews in the East'. And yet he had been 'sensitized in the highest degree' to the criminal nature of the Nazi regime in his family environment. The incredulity with which one reads this today is all the greater because it came to light in 2003 that Wapnewski had been listed in Nazi party membership rolls from the end of the 1930s. He claimed then too that he had not been aware of the fact.[4] Can such lapses of memory be authentic? That was another of the questions addressed by the participants in the conference. Micha Brumlik, born in 1947, had just discussed Claude Lanzmann's film *Shoah* in *Der Spiegel,* and he referred to the case of the chief railway inspector Walter Stier, who had been responsible in Cracow and Warsaw for the 'special transports' to Sobibor and Treblinka, but insisted to Lanzmann that he had known nothing about what was happening to the Jews. Brumlik thought even a perpetrator such as Stier must be assumed to have 'a certain subjective honesty' because 'there is such a deep-seated repression, such a deep-seated guilt, that subjectively honest answers of non-knowledge are possible'.

Habermas seems to have followed the discussion with growing agitation. Although he was – as he repeatedly stated – only an amateur among these professional historians, his interjections supplied crucial cues. His roughly outlined 'phases model' of West German commemorative culture, for example, saw a progression from a 'latent period' in the 1950s to a 'wave of discussion' in the 1960s, to the 'neo-conservative backlash' of the 1970s. As one of those 'born later', he listened in silence to the discussion of who had known what. Only when the historians weighed up the pros and cons of monuments and memorials did he speak out with an ardent appeal to preserve the vacuum of national symbols in West Germany. After the Nazis had taken the manipulation of the

collective memory to extremes, the Germans had a unique
historic opportunity to do 'without a model' – as Adorno's
1967 title put it – that is, without 'monuments, rituals, flags,
good God, all that nonsense' that had been used since the
nineteenth century to cultivate national identity. 'That was a
German opportunity to break once for all with the nationalism of the nineteenth century and take up an experimental,
pioneering role' – that is, to shape the 'rational identity' he
had spoken of in the early 1970s in Stuttgart in his Hegel Prize
acceptance speech.

Now, however, Habermas no longer seemed to assume that
such an identity could exist in the abstract – that is, as a mere
feeling of belonging to a community of communication based
on dominance-free discourse. In contrast to his earlier ideas,
the remembrance of the catastrophe had now moved into the
foreground; his republicanism, based on universalist principles, had taken on a historical tinge. What he imagined was
not a society without memory, but a remembrance without
symbols, which would reflect the 'discrediting' of the complex
of national tradition. 'After all, Auschwitz is a symbol for which
we have no monuments, fortunately, other than the hardware
that produced the whole thing.' And because this 'hardware'
was still to be found all over Germany, it was 'thank God
unnecessary to commission someone to make a monument'.

The historians were ready with their objections. Heinrich
August Winkler wanted an exception to Habermas's icono-
clasm at least for 'a minimum of republican symbols', such
as the black, red and gold '1848 flag'. Amos Funkenstein conceded he would 'in principle' advocate living without symbols,
'only I suspect that symbols are inevitable. Perhaps in an ideal
society it would be possible to do without them.' It was not
Habermas's intention at the *Wissenschaftskolleg* to conjure up
a utopian image of West Germany – far from it. In 1986, barely
forty years after the new German state had disappointed his
expectations for the first time, he brought up the motif of the

missed chance once more. But this time he was referring not to the distinction between 'formal' and 'material democracy' – that is, the question of political systems – but to the symbolic dimension. Thanks to the concerted action of the revisionists – the new tendencies in written history, Kohl's provocations, etc. – the whole experiment of post-national identity was teetering, Habermas thought. 'I would say,' he remarked sarcastically, 'we are well on the way to having, perhaps in twenty years, a homogenized interpretation under which we can relate to positive pasts, so that maybe we can even build monuments again.' He could not have guessed how accurate that prediction was – much less that he himself would be among the advocates of the monument which, twenty years later, would be a new model for the Germans' relation to their past.

What makes the records of Friedländer's conference so fascinating is the impression that we are witnessing a kind of dress rehearsal for the *Historikerstreit* that would soon take place – but a rehearsal held by only one of the two camps. At the end of the colloquium, Habermas gave free rein to his uneasiness. Although there was no consensus on a single one of the problems discussed, he observed in 'all German historians' an inclination towards 'de-dramatizing' and 'intra-disciplinary consensus-building', as well as a satisfaction about past achievements that left him 'incredibly annoyed'. Was this the moment of conception of his challenge to the whole discipline of history? Be that as it may, Habermas's tirade expressed the tension that lay over the whole event. But if the emotional chart showed such swings even among politically more or less like-minded people, what extremes of agitation would occur in the big interdisciplinary controversy he would open five months later?

Back in Starnberg, Habermas wrote to Friedländer – in April, that is, after an interval of several weeks – that the colloquium had 'stirred up a great deal, in each of us no doubt'. The previous evening he had watched Lanzmann's *Shoah*, which had finally been broadcast on public television in Bavaria, two months later than in the other West German states. In May, *Die Zeit* published a portrait of Friedländer in which he recounted the dinner at which Ernst Nolte confronted him with his thesis that the World Jewish Congress had declared war on Hitler's Germany. Friedländer is also cited in the *Die Zeit* article as mentioning another Berlin dinner with his hosts from the *Wissenschaftskolleg*, where a 'select' Moselle wine of 1943 vintage was served – after which the German professors, 'once they were properly full of cheer', sang the popular song *Theo, wir fahr'n nach Lodz*. Łódź had been the first stop on the way to the death camps for Berlin's Jews transported from Grunewald station. But far from assuming any ill intentions on the part of his colleagues, Friedländer was merely amazed at the degree of repression that still seemed to be normal even among the educational elite of West Germany. Because of the scandals that had occurred during his time in Berlin, however – the Fassbinder play *Der Müll, die Stadt und der Tod* ['Rubbish, the city and death']; the remark by a Christian-Democrat mayor that it was time to 'beat a few rich Jews to death' to refloat the municipal finances – Friedländer predicted 'a new general debate' about the Germans' handling of their repressed past. Three weeks later, Nolte's article appeared in the *Frankfurter Allgemeine Zeitung* – and the rest is history.[5]

# Stirrings of Post-National Feeling

The West Germans, Habermas wrote in the spring of 1990, had been caught completely off guard by the opening of the Berlin Wall. We may read that as autobiographical. The sheer amazement is still audible in his voice today as he tells me, in the course of our talk in Starnberg, about the night of 9 November 1989, when he sat before the television set in Frankfurt together with his wife and a few friends from Suhrkamp circles. It is significant that the impulsive thinker waited weeks before writing his first reaction to the epoch-making event, and then it was only for the private public sphere of his own acquaintances. The end of East Germany – to say nothing of the reunification of the two German states – had not been among the political events he could have anticipated. 'We would have to conclude that we must no longer want that', the SPD member Heinrich August Winkler had said about the restoration of a German nation-state at the 1986 *Wissenschaftskolleg* conference – a conclusion that Habermas himself had long since drawn without the contortions of the conditional mood. He had rejected German unity since the end of the war, when it was still a project of the left, and spurned it all the more after it had been co-opted by the opposite camp.[1]

Habermas's stock-taking of his relationship to East Germany now, after the fall of the regime, was accordingly sober, almost curt. As a student in the early 1950s, he had been to the Theater am Schiffbauerdamm a few times to see Brecht's productions, and later as a member of the University of Bonn's film club he had borrowed DEFA films from an East Berlin office of the communist youth organization FDJ. His first visit to East Germany after that was not until the summer of 1988, when he gave a lecture at the invitation of a colleague at the University of Halle in the overflowing main auditorium there. 'Those days were instructive to me and my wife, but the German Democratic Republic was already mentally broken down by then. We left rather depressed, and skipped our planned stop in Weimar.' Between those visits: three and a half decades with no relationship at all. No official contacts, no visits to relatives, no communication with oppositional groups – except for the fact that the East German songwriter Wolf Biermann came to Starnberg for a few days after his expatriation in November of 1976. 'He knew nothing about me and I knew nothing about him', Biermann later recalled in regard to this meeting. 'We amiably talked right over each other's heads.' Apart from that, Habermas's papers contain nothing but a six-page letter from a psychology student in East Berlin who had asked him in 1986 for intellectual support. The philosopher had conscientiously tried to answer all the questions put to him. The copy of *The Theory of Communicative Action* that he posted separately was confiscated by the East German authorities.[2]

As he freely admitted, Habermas was in the same situation as Frankfurt's Social Democratic cultural affairs commissioner Linda Reisch, whose remark that she knew more about Milan than Leipzig had been widely reported in the summer of 1990. Habermas: 'It's something you have to grasp without sentimentalism.' After all, on their 1988 trip he and his wife had declined to pay homage to the city where Goethe had lived and worked. In 1991, the idea, current among conservative politicians and intellectuals, of restoring a continuum of German intellectual history by reconnecting with Weimar and Jena, was to him 'land-grabbing territorial fetishism'. The weakness for national commemorative sites, a concept of the French historian Pierre Nora that had gained surprising popularity since the mid-1980s, was a manifestation of an obsolete mentality.[3]

Overnight, the prospect of reunification transformed the intellectuals' trench warfare of the 1980s – the disputes about attitudes towards the past, collective memory and German identity – into urgent political issues. An exemplary indicator of that change is the fate of a friendship that did not survive the tectonic shifts of 1990. In hindsight, it is little wonder; the wonder is, rather, that the friendship between Habermas and Karl Heinz Bohrer lasted as long as it did. Perhaps such friendships could only thrive in the safe space of the old West Germany. Their falling out, with its private and its public aspects, may stand for the chasm that opened up in the 1990s within the German intelligentsia. Since the late 1960s they had met, sometimes more regularly, sometimes sporadically, to cultivate the contrast between their intellectual temperaments – united by a partiality to modernity and to the West as an 'emotional compass point'. Right up to his death, Bohrer never tired of repeating that he valued Habermas as an interlocutor who, impulsively and with argumentative finesse, defended the cause of reason – against which Bohrer insisted on his right to an untamed aesthetic subjectivity.[4]

The excitement of their wine-fuelled discussions may have been that of an ongoing intellectual duel to the philosophical aristocrat Bohrer, and that of an athletic contest to the competitive Habermas. Bohrer was the only one, Habermas had written in 1979, before he had begun hunting down the renegades of modernity, 'who has preserved, in a politically innocent and sovereign manner, something of the radicalness and neoromantic intelligence of a young-conservative' – and he meant it as a compliment! Bohrer's appeal for Germany 'as an intellectual option', published the same year in the *Frankfurter Allgemeine Zeitung*, cannot have been to Habermas's taste, nor can his derision of the peace movement, his interest in the postmodern French or his opening series as the new editor of *Merkur*, in which he focused on the provinciality and ugliness of the Bonn republic. As with Walser, though, Habermas had long overlooked such differences. During the *Historikerstreit*, in fact, their shared aversion to Helmut Kohl and his obtuse historicism had brought Habermas and Bohrer politically closer once more. 'I fully agree with your essay', Bohrer had assured Habermas after his criticism of Nolte – but not without adding that there was 'not only a fundamentalist-historicist "interpretation", but also a universalist-rational' one, and that Bohrer, as a Romantic, was sceptical of both.[5]

In June 1989, Habermas had invited his friend to his sixtieth birthday in a Bavarian inn. Six months later, their fragile relationship was thrown off balance: after the Wall fell, Bohrer quickly came to the conclusion that unification with West Germany was both desirable and unavoidable for the crumbling German Democratic Republic. Like his sparring partner, however, he too was worried about forfeiting credibility by a premature judgement. It is nonetheless surprising that he chose Habermas to read the draft of the essay he was writing for the *Frankfurter Allgemeine Zeitung*. How could he have thought the philosopher would be even remotely sympathetic? It must have been plain to Bohrer that what he criticized as the anti-unification Germans' narrow-minded 'mentality of teachers, pedagogues and pastors' matched Habermas's attitude exactly.[6]

Bohrer's appeal to shake off the 'colonized consciousness' and reverse the 'highly neurotic self-destruction of the Germans as a nation' amounted to a choice between a stuffy, provincial Germany and a cosmopolitan, urbane one – a choice that led him a year and a half later to advocate strongly for the proposal to move the seat of government to Berlin. The desire to keep East Germany as 'a kind of nature sanctuary for socially and economically dreamed-of yesterdays' and West Germany as an apolitical feel-good oasis was to Bohrer a return to the tradition of German mini-states, complete with blinkers, narrow-mindedness and vassal mentality – that is, the same provincialism that he had written about as early as the 1980s. Although Bohrer's moves from Frankfurt, where they had first met, to London and then Paris and Habermas's move to his bungalow in Starnberg were dictated by the contingencies of their respective careers, those life choices seem in retrospect to express political and cultural preferences.[7]

In his memoirs, Bohrer recalls that Habermas begged him not to publish his text. It didn't matter that the idea of a constitutional patriotism came off relatively well in his reflections as the 'most sublime variation of the tabooization of the nation', which one day might even prove to be the seed of a post-national myth – Habermas found 'entirely erroneous' the idea that the Germans had atoned for the crimes of Nazism by the loss of East Prussia and Silesia. Most importantly, however, his own assessment of West Germany was diametrically opposed to Bohrer's. The very fact that West German police officers, in their beige and green polyester uniforms, looked like 'armed toilet attendants', or that the Bonn Republic did without an imposing national capital – the very fact that West Germany, as Gustav Seibt wrote, had become by the late 1980s 'one of the most undistinguished states in history' – Habermas, like many on the left, saw these supposed shortcomings as historic achievements. The West Germany of the late 1980s seems to have been almost a kind of tangible utopia to him. He had initially expected the worst from the Kohl government, and had ended up in another skirmish with the conservative members of his generation in the *Historikerstreit*, but now the wind had changed again during the unspectacular parliamentary election campaign of 1987.[8]

While the rise of Rita Süssmuth signalled that the Christian Democrats had been pulled along in the slipstream of the country's 'fundamental liberalization' since 1968, and while the left 'to the left of the Social Democrats' showed signs of identifying with constitutional institutions, social scientists' surveys indicated that the post-national mentality was now beginning to prevail in the broader population as well. True, the term *Politikverdrossenheit,* or 'disenchantment with politics', was gaining currency at the same time. Would Habermas perhaps have turned to a new career in alternative medicine if the *posthistoire* of the Kohl era had crystallized into a permanent state? In any case, the fall of the Wall on 9 November took him completely by surprise. Just as 'behavioural therapy' – Jan Philipp Reemtsma's term for West German history – had begun to bear fruit; just as the country, and not only its cities, had finally 'become a contemporary of Western Europe' after forty years, and its left-wing intellectuals were set for quieter times, its long-past history as a nation-state was threatening to catch up with it.[9]

Bohrer had to admit, to his surprise, that his and Habermas's positions could 'not be farther apart'. To Habermas, unification was – in Bohrer's words – the epitome of 'political disaster', and so Bohrer's article, published in spite of Habermas's objections in January of 1990 in the *Frankfurter Allgemeine Zeitung* under the title 'Why We Are Not a Nation: And Why We Should Become One', was an affront. At first Bohrer expressed the hope 'that our personal relations are more secure in theoretical than in political discussion'. Later he announced he would 'do everything to prevent a definitive rupture' – and urged Habermas to make the effort to de-escalate as well: 'Not only I am extremely impulsive on occasion: you are, too.' But the political gulf could no longer be bridged – not even after Habermas admitted that German unification was inevitable. His last letter to Bohrer is dated October 1990, after the die had been cast. It marked the end not only of a twenty-year intellectual friendship, but also of Habermas's contributions to *Merkur*, in which he had published more than forty articles since the early 1950s. It would have been intriguing to see the article on 'historicity' that Bohrer had tried to persuade him to write. But Habermas was not even willing to contribute a piece for the eightieth birthday of the former editor-in-chief Hans Paeschke, nor did he ever publish in *Merkur* again.[10]

At the time, I followed the debates about reunification only at a distance. I went to the United States as an exchange student in January of 1990. As I can see from photos from that year, I too transformed temporarily into an American. Only in the summer after my return, six months before my eighteenth birthday, did I begin reading *Die Zeit* and *Frankfurter Rundschau* regularly. Those were the newspapers my parents subscribed to, and those were the papers in which Habermas commented on current events. In the yellowed files of clippings that I collected in the early 1990s, I come across his articles on German unity, on the Gulf War and on the debate over political asylum – the first texts of his I ever read.

As I realize on re-reading them, he must have seen the reunification of Germany as a test case for the theory of constitutional democracy that he had been working on since the mid-1980s. His critique was aimed first of all against the chancellor's 'policy of speed', as the unification that Kohl was pursuing would be merely an administrative act under West Germany's putatively provisional 1949 constitution, whose Article 23 defines how new states may join the Federal Republic. Habermas considered that a pan-German state required for its legitimacy an act of public deliberation – more specifically, a pan-German constitutional assembly. At the same time, however, he conceded little leeway to the East Germans as to the possible results of such an assembly. The thought experiment of a 'third way' between a market economy and state socialism, which briefly seemed to be an option after the Wall fell, was no longer relevant to Habermas once the CDU had won the Eastern parliamentary elections in March of 1990. The term with which he summarized the events – the 'rectifying revolution' – indicates his feeling that its direction was predetermined. A revolution with a 'total lack of ideas that are either innovative or orientated towards the future' would end up reproducing the Western status quo at best.[11]

'It would surprise me very much', Habermas wrote to Christa Wolf, with whom he had a brief correspondence in 1991, 'if there were any difference of opinion between us about which traditions we wish to continue.' The GDR, he wrote, which had had neither a re-education nor a 1968, seemed to have conserved 'something of the mentality of the thirties and forties'. In this situation, didn't constitutional patriotism require West Germany to defend against the illiberal influence of that mentality? In one of the articles I cut out in those days, Habermas expressed the fear that the abuse of progressive ideas in actually existing socialism could be 'more ruinous for the spiritual hygiene of Germany than all the concentrated resentment of five or six generations of anti-Enlightenment, anti-Semitic, false Romantic, jingoistic obscurantists' – in other words, more disastrous than the intellectual legacy of Nazism. When he called such ruin a second 'destruction of reason', was he thinking of the destruction of the old West Germany? The Habermas of the early 1990s turns out to have been a truly post-national thinker. Looking back on the reunification of Germany from his perspective, one gets the impression the West German state had been facing the task of integrating the population of a remote Asian dictatorship in its political culture.[12]

Understandably, the East German intellectuals were disconcerted. To Christa Wolf, Habermas's fear of her unenlightened compatriots revealed a dismaying ignorance. The East Berlin author Friedrich Dieckmann considered the 'Rhenish separatism' of the West German left not only illusory, but openly cynical: 'As if one fourth of the German people had to go on living in a state that was economically crumbling, sinking to the level of a developing country, just so that three-fourths of the nation could feel shielded from the evils of German national history.' Dieckmann saw the self-satisfaction of the post-national West Germany as the counterpart to the faded doctrine of the East German politburo which had declared the GDR the state of antifascist resistance: the same cautionary reference to Nazism was used to bolster the comfortable status quo of the West German intelligentsia in the one case and the East German nomenklatura in the other.[13]

Since then, we have learned, however, that Habermas was right to have his fears. That the 'republicans of habit' among the West German liberal-conservatives would turn into national conservatives, as he had prophesied at the end of 1989, was evident three years later in the debate on Botho Strauss's essay in *Der Spiegel*, 'Swelling Goat-Song' ['*Anschwellender Bocksgesang*'], which the new intellectual right chose as its manifesto. A new nationalism has since become established in Germany, spanning all social classes and milieus, and is reshaping the spectrum of political parties. The underpinning of representative democracy in the no longer new states of the Federal Republic is thin as measured today – November 2023 – in the forecasts for the coming state parliamentary elections in Thuringia and Saxony. Although this challenge to the republic's legitimacy is in keeping with an international trend, it may have been significantly strengthened by the arrogance of West German elites. To borrow Habermas's diction, we might see this as a dialectic of de-legitimation – one to which he himself contributed, in a way. It would not be too much to say that Habermas, who insisted on seeing the historical import of 1989 under the shadow of 1945, became the philosophical representative of the Berlin Republic only insofar as it is the continuation of its Bonn predecessor.[14]

# The Primacy of Global
# Domestic Politics

One of the axioms of social history is what is called the primacy of domestic politics: the belief that the principal actions in history can be considered as being merely reflections of internal social structures. As we have seen in the previous chapters, Habermas the intellectual restricted himself for a long time to a West German point of view; the democratization of his compatriots – and even the country's integration in the West – was to him mainly a domestic, German problem. A telling example is the anthology he edited in 1979, *Stichworte zur geistigen Situation der Zeit* [partially translated as *Observations on 'The Spiritual Situation of the Age'*]: it would be unthinkable today to write a diagnosis of the present in which the world beyond the borders is all but unmentioned. 'I've never been a fan of the idea of a "unified Europe"', Habermas explained that same year, adding, 'even when it was fashionable.' As a Marxist, he had rejected the Adenauer project of the European Economic Community as an agency of international capitalism.[1]

Only after the historic end of the experiment known as West Germany did Europe become a point of reference to Habermas – and in fact his 'main current preoccupation' in the noughties, as he confessed in 2006 on accepting the

Bruno Kreisky Prize for political writing. Alongside the advances of the new German commemorative politics, which took its present shape over the course of the 1990s, he saw the absorption of Germany into a supranational community as life insurance against the new German nationalism. 'In Germany we need the political union, if only to protect us from ourselves', he declared in 1993, after the Maastricht agreement had been signed the previous year. In Habermas's political calculus, the EU was in many respects the continuation of Germany's Western integration by other means.[2]

The rocky European road to unity can be recapitulated through Habermas's successive commentaries: from the introduction of the euro to the eastward enlargement of the EU and the failure of the constitutional referenda in France and the Netherlands, to the Treaty of Lisbon and the euro crisis triggered by the crash of 2008. In every phase, at every course adjustment, he repeated his call to 'deepen' the EU, overcome its democratic deficits and more precisely define its political goals. That included not only fencing in a globally unfettered capitalism by means of a coordinated European financial policy, but also – after the 'earthquake unleashed by the illegal Iraq policy of the Bush administration' – keeping Europe from falling into the helpless role of 'Uncle Sam's poodle' by means of an autonomous foreign policy and security policy. Habermas saw no alternative to this agenda in the 'post-national constellation', in which nation-states were reduced to 'the format of former princedoms'.[3]

It is surprising how logically, almost compellingly, Habermas's notions of European politics followed from the ideas of post-national identity, constitutional patriotism and deliberative democracy – the ideas that had formed the focus of his thinking since the mid-1980s and were now refracted as if through a prism by the global watershed of 1989/90 and its aftermath. In this respect, Habermas is once more the philosopher of the old West Germany, having continuously adapted and updated his theoretical toolbox, but not fundamentally replaced it, since that country ended. 'When you are sixty,' Gadamer had once written to him – from his own experience – 'you don't learn anything new any more.' But maybe there was nothing substantial left for Habermas to learn. Even before the fall of East Germany, he had expressed – in an acceptance speech in Copenhagen – the hope that 'more general issues' could be found in the German special case. Not a bad phrase to describe what had been occupying him, the thinker from the 'universal provinces', since the 1990s.[4]

The end of the Cold War opened up a broad field of applications for his concepts. If citizenship in a democracy was not rooted in a primordial national identity, if such an identity formed rather in the course of deliberative processes of communication, then there was no reason to doubt that a comparable development could be repeated on the supranational level. Hence the importance that Habermas attached to the project of a European constitution. He hoped that the debate that must precede a constitutional treaty would give birth to a European public sphere, which in turn would become the germ of a European identity. In view of the continent's ethnic and cultural heterogeneity, that identity would necessarily be a constitutional patriotism. Those who complained that the project of a united Europe could not claim to be founded on a European people, Habermas objected, were clinging to the essentialist way of thinking of the nineteenth century and refusing to understand the recursive nature of collective identity formation.[5]

Habermas's willingness to see the future potential of the new situation after every setback that the process of European unity has suffered since the millennium once again displays his talent, nourished by historical experience, for reacting with optimism to missed opportunities. Jan Philipp Reemtsma, in his commendatory speech on the awarding of the German Publishers' Association's 2001 Peace Prize to Habermas, identified 'connectability' as the central theme of his work. By that he meant not only the philosopher's technique of grafting his own theories onto the classic texts, but also the ethos that Habermas had developed of 'responsibility for the continuation of a process' – in contrast to the contrariness of Critical Theory: precisely because the process is stripped of all historical determinism, there is no alternative but to make sure something 'comes next'. *Weitermachen!*, 'Carry on!', is engraved on Herbert Marcuse's tombstone in the Dorotheenstadt cemetery in Berlin, a maxim that Habermas too seems to have adopted, their contrasting political temperaments notwithstanding. 'It's no use crying over spilled milk', he once said in an interview after the German unification – otherwise he couldn't do anything but keep the 'diary of a Hellenistic writer who merely documents, for subsequent generations, the unfulfilled promises of his waning culture'.[6]

But Habermas's optimism can also be seen as legitimatory thinking, making even the most unpleasant status quo bearable in light of the Idea – which is hardly distinguishable from the attitude of a Right Hegelian. As late as 2007, he had warned that the Treaty of Lisbon, which called for a council of national governments as the executive branch of the EU, would abandon the principle of supranational unity and decide 'the future of the European Union' in favour of 'the neoliberal orthodoxy'; but after the treaty's ratification he praised the new order 'as an important stage along the route to a politically constituted world society'. In nonchalantly elevating a skill such as 'learning from other cultures' to a premise of European convergence, in remarking *en passant* that the Europeans' political self-image must develop from now on only 'through a non-pejorative differentiation from the citizens of other continents', he sounded thoroughly homiletic. Was it not at least equally likely that the continent would gain its cohesion – if at all – out of fear of growing streams of refugees, or, later, out of mobilization against Putin's Russia? Perry Anderson, a critic of Europe from the left who compared Habermas's collection of awards with a Soviet general's uniform, sees the philosopher as a victim of his own success. 'Often hailed as a contemporary successor to Kant,' Anderson wrote in 2012, 'he risks becoming a modern Leibniz, constructing with imperturbable euphemisms a theodicy in which even the evils of financial deregulation contribute to the blessings of cosmopolitan awakening, while the West sweeps the path of democracy and human rights towards an ultimate Eden of pan-human legitimacy.'[7]

At one time Helmut Kohl had helped him to make peace with the old West Germany, but in 1998 the Red–Green coalition government granted Habermas actual access to power. He had his former auditing student Joschka Fischer to thank for that privilege, having kept up a loose dialogue with him since the mid-1980s – although Habermas still considers himself a left-wing Social Democrat, and never abandoned his scepticism towards the Greens, the party that had grown out of the alternative movement of the '70s. In spite of his public influence, Habermas has long felt himself to be a leftist underdog, but in 1999 – ten years after a critic had called his discourse-theoretical philosophy of law 'anarchistic' – he was handed the Theodor Heuss Prize for exemplary democratic demeanour, and he had to admit that he had arrived 'in the centre of our society'. That same year, Habermas, alongside the Green foreign minister Fischer, supported the NATO mission in Kosovo – the Bundeswehr's first mission outside Germany. In the summer of 2001, the two joined forces again to promote a European constitution. Habermas sees the conferment of the Peace Prize of the German Publishers' Association four months later as the zenith of his public career – and in fact the *Frankfurter Allgemeine Zeitung* declared him a 'pop star' and *Die Zeit* the 'Hegel of the Federal Republic'. Although he assures me emphatically that he never saw himself as the 'state's philosopher', he does not hide his satisfaction at the fact that the award ceremony in St Paul's

Church in Frankfurt was attended by Chancellor Schröder's entire cabinet.[8]

Although his ties to the political establishment have since grown looser again, it is still *bon ton* among leading Social Democrats today to profess to read Habermas. With his faith in the power of communication, the German president Frank-Walter Steinmeier is the most prominent representative of the tradition of discourse theory. During his time as the SPD chairman and German foreign minister, Sigmar Gabriel regularly sought Habermas's advice. And even Olaf Scholz, who confessed in an interview in the *Süddeutsche Zeitung* in the summer of 2023 how little use he has today for the Marxist theories he 'dug through' as a Young Social Democrat, added an important qualification to that change of heart: 'Except for Habermas: I got a lot out of him, both in those days and today.'[9]

# On War

In the same newspaper, the philosopher had lent the chancellor his support with his statements on the war in Ukraine. Faltering weapons deliveries and continued dependency on Russian gas had given rise in the spring of 2022 to a debate on Germany's future international role – indeed, its very identity. Habermas defended Scholz's hesitant course as a strategy to prevent escalation. He evoked the danger of nuclear war and recalled that Putin had the 'asymmetrical advantage' of being able to choose at what point he would see the Western allies as belligerents. In a second article in early 2023, Habermas advocated pressing for negotiations with Russia while at the same time supporting Ukraine militarily. But mainly he criticized the 'war-mongering rhetoric' of the 'morally outraged' German public, which in his eyes rested on a 'confusion of historically discontinuous mentalities'. After the Second World War, the 'post-heroic' consciousness had formed in Germany 'that international conflicts can only be solved through diplomacy and sanctions'. A younger generation that had no experience of war identified with the Ukrainians' spirit of sacrifice and confidence of victory, after the Russian invasion had knocked Ukraine back to a historically earlier phase of nation-building.

To Habermas, that was a dangerous failure to recognize a hard-won standard of civilization, as was the rhetoric of 'changing times'.[1]

Habermas's two articles unleashed a storm of indignation. The reactions mentioned an 'attitude of submission', an 'escalation phobia' and a 'schoolmasterly appeal for moderation'. According to the American historian Timothy Snyder, Habermas was arguing 'from the perspective of a sentimentalized West Germany of the 1970s'. The former ambassador and vice-foreign minister of Ukraine, Andriy Melnyk, tweeted about a 'disgrace to German philosophy': Kant and Hegel would 'turn in their graves for shame'. Snyder even accused Habermas of anti-Semitism because he had warned that Zelensky's masterly use of media could be manipulative. More circumspect critics recalled that Habermas had always been insensitive to the political strivings of the East Europeans, and found his proposal unrealistic, since Putin showed no willingness to negotiate. Across the political spectrum, from the cultural section of the *FAZ* to the Twitter bubbles of the post-migration left, the philosopher was accused of sticking his head in the self-referential sand of old West German 'national pacifism', blind to the new global situation.[2]

And in fact, pacifist motifs have always played a part in Habermas's thought and action. In the 1950s, he demonstrated against nuclear weapons for the Bundeswehr; in the 1960s, he took the podium against the Vietnam War; and although he abstained from joining in human chains in the 1980s, he contributed to the legitimation of protests against the NATO Double-Track Decision with a defence of civil disobedience grounded in democratic political theory. 'The experience of the war had made me a pacifist', he explained in a 1979 interview. He held to his belief in the 'obsolescence of war as a category in world history' even after the caesura of 1989, although he arrived at a more nuanced position in the new geopolitical situation. In 1991 too, during the Second Gulf

War, he advocated a German 'policy of restraint', as he would do later in the case of the Ukraine war. It was Helmut Kohl who had preferred to support the coalition against Saddam Hussein with funds rather than sending German fighter jets to the Gulf. Hans Magnus Enzensberger's comparison of Saddam with Hitler was to Habermas – once again – the 'crazy hypothesis' of an intellectual who could not be taken seriously as a political analyst. The 'politics of radical pacifism' was not to be swallowed whole either, however. In particular, Habermas demanded unconditional support for Israel, which Saddam was threatening to reduce to 'a crematorium' with his Scud missiles. 'There can be worse evils than war,' Habermas wrote in *Die Zeit* a month after the beginning of Operation Desert Storm, in an article that left no doubt as to the legality per se of an intervention in Iraq sanctioned by a UN mandate. That sentence leads in a straight line to the qualification Habermas formulated with regard to the Ukraine war: scepticism against military force ends where the price to be paid is that of a 'life stifled by authoritarianism'.[3]

One indication of how strongly the field of debate in Germany has changed since then is the fact that the most vehement critique of his position in 1991 came from the peace movement. 'In 1968, Habermas still recognized the character of US imperialism in Vietnam', says one of the many letters to the editor of *Die Zeit*. 'Today, in 1991, he no longer sees that the war in the Gulf serves only the purpose of defending the strategic interests of American capitalism.' Habermas was of course not so naive as to overlook the context of power politics. In the unilateral moment of the 1990s, however, he nurtured the hope that America's characteristic foreign policy, a 'hybrid of humanitarian altruism and the imperial logic of power', could permit a leap into a new global order. As early as the Gulf War, Habermas saw the West in 'the (presumably neutral) role of police force to the United Nations – a force that is still lacking to this day'. He felt the time had come, after the end of the Cold War, to realize that 'situation of world citizenship' that Kant had mentioned as early as the eighteenth century – that is, to institutionalize a worldwide human rights policy transcending classic international law.[4]

In another front page article in *Die Zeit* in the spring of 1999, Habermas expressed his approval of the NATO mission in Kosovo – the first Bundeswehr mission outside Germany – even though the allies could not claim a UN mandate this time because of the Russian veto. Habermas went on to sketch the scenario of a 'thoroughly legalized cosmopolitan order' whose maintenance would not require a world government, but merely the coordination of a functioning Security Council with the new International Criminal Court in The Hague and an international police force. Unlike the conventional pacifism 'of conviction', the 'legal pacifism' associated with such an order would not be a moralization of politics in which 'violations of basic human rights are evaluated and fought in an unmediated way according to philosophical *moral* standards'. Rather, such violations would then be 'prosecuted as criminal acts within a state-ordained *legal* order'. During the Gulf War, Habermas had revisited the concept of 'global domestic policy' coined by Carl Friedrich von Weizsäcker in the 1960s, and found the primacy of domestic politics as valid as ever in the new global age.[5]

This time, however, criticism came not only from the pacifist camp. In his appeal for the authorization of the international organizations, the philosopher seemed to be ignoring the very fact that NATO was operating in Kosovo without a UN mandate, as if that were merely a cosmetic flaw. The bombing of Belgrade was 'beyond any possible justification', his colleague Reinhard Merkel reproached him in *Die Zeit*. The legal scholar Dieter Simon took issue with the 'missionary zeal of Enlightenment universalism', which closed its eyes to the 'monstrosity of war as an elementary crime'. And while the peace researcher Lutz Schrader suspected that Habermas's judgement had been clouded by his association with the Green foreign minister Fischer, Peter Handke – taking the side of Serbia – saw Habermas's opinion as nothing but a 'defence of mindless violence'.[6]

In retrospect, we can make at least one observation: as far as the question of German participation in military interventions since the end of the Cold War is concerned, Habermas supported the position of the sitting German government not only in the case of Kosovo in 1999, but in every other case as well. In that respect, he does indeed prove to be loyal to the state. The same is true of his position on the third Gulf War, which – one and a half years after 9/11 – began with the invasion of Iraq by American and British ground troops in March of 2003. Germany and France had by that time defected from the 'coalition of the willing', drawing Donald Rumsfeld's contemptuous comment about 'Old Europe'. In April, after the conquest of Baghdad, Habermas took stock of the situation in a scathing essay in the *Frankfurter Allgemeine Zeitung*. He mentioned the CIA's torture methods, the violation of the Geneva Conventions in Guantánamo, and the Bush administration's disinformation campaign connecting Saddam Hussein with Osama bin Laden. But the gravest offence, to him, was the contempt for international law shown by the American war of aggression. In the 'Bush Doctrine', developed long before 9/11, Habermas saw more than the cynicism of a superpower: it was a revolution in American foreign policy, 'an unimaginable break with norms that the United States had been committed to'. And still more drastically: 'Let us have no illusions: the normative authority of the United States of America lies in ruins.'[7]

Coming from a philosopher for whom America had been a normative authority throughout his lifetime, this was a momentous statement. As early as October 2001, having gone to New York University in the traumatized metropolis just a month after the attack on the World Trade Center, Habermas had 'somehow felt more of a stranger than on any previous visit'.

The American cosmopolitanism, 'the impressive American generosity toward foreigners' that he had first encountered in the 1960s, seemed to have given way to a general mistrust. Would 'we who had not been present . . . now also stand by them unconditionally'?[8]

The mutual estrangement that Habermas noted here for the first time grew in his eyes over the course of subsequent events into a gulf dividing the West. The 'war on terrorism' not only shook his political geography, but also rearranged his philosophical map. The very country to which the Germans owed their bond with Western civilization breaking with the Western tradition of thought must be counted as one of the greatest intellectual disasters of his life. In consequence, the project of European unity became nothing less than a question of political survival. Habermas, still hopeful in spite of everything, saw the demonstrations – 'the largest since the end of World War II' – that had taken place in several European capitals in February of 2003, shortly before the American invasion of Iraq, as the self-assertion of that 'Old Europe' that Rumsfeld relegated to the dung-heap of history. The manifesto that Habermas published a short time later together with Jacques Derrida and other European intellectuals – putting aside their earlier differences – appealed to the Europeans to consider what they had in common with each other, and not with America, and to create the institutions that would be required for a symbolic, mentality-building European foreign policy as a counterweight to the 'hegemonic unilateralism' of the United States.[9]

Today, twenty years later, there is still no trace of an autonomous, unified European foreign policy. The Europeans' response to Russian aggression has consisted of scrambling for the safety of NATO's American shield, and in the most severe Middle East crisis since the Yom Kippur War, the EU has likewise proved unable to play any significant political role. But the hope Habermas had expressed as recently as

2003 that the USA could 'once again [position] itself at the forefront as the driving force', acting as the avant-garde of a politics of human rights, has also gone unfulfilled. Neither Obama's inconstant foreign policy nor Trump's erratic presidency was likely to repair the image of a superpower plagued by internal crises. In November 2023, as I write these lines, a House of Representatives dominated by the radical wing of the Republican Party is blocking the next deliveries of weapons to Ukraine, and demanding drastic concessions in domestic policy in return for its approval of military aid to Israel.[10]

'The clock is ticking for the Biden administration', Habermas wrote in January 2023 in his appeal for negotiations with Russia. The Americans have long since ceased to be a reliable partner. Although the heat of the debate may have suggested otherwise, the remarkable thing about Habermas's comments on the Ukraine war was not their supposed pacifism or defeatism, but the implication that he had lost his faith in the possibility of global domestic politics. It is not as if he hadn't had second thoughts before. '[W]hat do we say', he had written as early as 1999, 'when one day the military alliance of another region – for example, in Asia – pursues the politics of human rights by military means in accordance with a very different interpretation of international law or the UN charter?' Such a situation is – from the Russian perspective – a reality today. Habermas too evidently sees no party today that is acting 'on behalf of the common interest'. 'From an enlightened postcolonial perspective, the West is no longer in a position to make loudmouthed normative appeals to a human-rights order that it has violated itself to persuade neutral powers like India, Brazil and South Africa to take sides in support of Ukraine', he said in an interview in *Granta* in the summer of 2023. The demand to bring the war criminal Putin to The Hague now seems to him the expression of a naive ethics of moral conviction. 'How deeply upturned must be the soil of our political culture . . . on which our children and grandchildren live, if even the conservative

press is calling for the prosecutors of an International Criminal
Court which has not yet been recognized by Russia and China,
or even by the US?'[11]

Indeed, how drastically the coordinates have shifted since
the 1990s is indicated by the very fact that this head-shaking
comes from Habermas himself, who played a major part in
formulating the norms of the Annalena Baerbock generation.
Today, he almost seems surprised that he was ever taken seriously, and argues more like one of the 'hard-nosed' realists
who were his closest enemies throughout his lifetime. 'Even
if we admit that universal Social Democracy is the only way
humanity can survive today,' Leo Strauss wrote to him back
in 1964, 'we must not overlook the power of that democracy's
enemies, that is, Russia and China.' Does Habermas see it as
his task today, sixty years later, to pass on this warning to the
next generation?[12]

# The Philosopher of the
# Universal Provinces

In September 2023, I went back to Starnberg – almost a year and a half after my first visit. This time the route was served by buses from Gauting onwards due to maintenance work on the tracks. The trip along the highway took significantly longer. We rode through forests and lush pastures, passed mountain bikers in outdoor gear, approached Starnberg through a stately old residential district where the prosperous citizens of Munich began settling at the turn of the twentieth century. Interspersed between the alluring Jugendstil mansions are modern architect-designed bungalows in exposed concrete and larchwood. If there is any place in Germany that still looks as though all's right with the world, this is it.

This time I know the ritual of making tea and small talk in the kitchen, followed by the walk to the sofa corner, where we switch from interaction to discourse. My intensive reading of Habermas has raised many questions, but most of all I haven't been able to forget our previous talk, at the end of which the philosopher expressed his dismay at the German discussion on the war. Since then, two of his contemporaries whom we talked about then, Enzensberger and Walser, have died. The transformation of the German mentality seems to be continuing unabated. As if to illustrate Habermas's worst fears, the author Rainald Goetz has written that he was finally able to 'really sympathize with the historical moment of August 1914, the collective willingness to go to war; this is how the people in those days experienced it, how they ran all over Europe into this Great War, out of the kind of mood that now hinted at arising again'. Meanwhile the Social Democrat minister of defence, Boris Pistorius, alluded to the spectre of a 'war in Europe', and may even have meant a war on German soil: not just the Bundeswehr, but German society too, he said, must be made 'ready'.[1]

Habermas, on the other hand, clings with growing desperation to his belief that efforts to reach a ceasefire and the search for a negotiated settlement to the conflict with Russia are absolutely necessary. He perceives the 'war mood' of the German public as background music to a disastrous strategic miscalculation that could prove to be a geopolitical turning point. I would like to hear what he would advise the chancellor to do now, in the autumn of 2023, but first he fleshes out the gloomy scenario of the decline of the West, which for him is inseparable from the decline of the political institutions in the United States. He talks about the division of American society and the 'collapse of the two-party system', which Trump has made impossible to ignore, but which was foreshadowed by the increasing polarization of the late 1990s. Habermas thinks the disruption of the political institutions is so severe that their legitimacy has been damaged for a long time to come. His wife, who has joined us for a while this time too, has long criticized him for 'idealizing' the US. But evidently he has gone through a painful process to overcome that attitude. It strikes me as symbolic that his Reeboks, after a year of use, don't look quite so brilliantly white today.[2]

As far as Ukraine is concerned, Habermas prophesies a gradual withdrawal of the Americans as soon as the war turns out to be political ballast in Biden's re-election campaign. And he fears that the ensuing decay of the coalition of supporters will cost the West the last vestiges of political credibility and authority that it still has. For he no longer believes that Europe will still blossom into a 'globally influential' actor – not since the failure of Emmanuel Macron's initiatives in that direction. His former hopes for cosmopolitan conditions have gone the same way: 'That's all yesterday's news.' And then Habermas says a sentence that stops the flow of our conversation for a moment: everything that constituted his life is now being lost, 'step by step'. He would not be the fighter he is if he did not steel himself in the same breath against the arrogance of those who always thought they knew better: 'It's too easy to make fun of such idealism in retrospect. No contemporary historian worth their salt would write history exclusively from the cynical perspective of the disappointing outcomes.' It is disturbing to hear Habermas – the last idealist – sounding so fatalistic. Is there nothing left for him in the end but the role of the 'Hellenistic writer' memorializing the 'unfulfilled promises of his waning culture' for future generations?[3]

Acquiescing once more to my request, he recapitulates episodes of his biography. He tells about the immediate postwar years, when he had to 'read up' on how a democracy works, as if all that were much more recent than the geopolitical illusions of the late 1990s; about Gershom Scholem's sobering presence, which made even Ernst Bloch subdued; about the suspenseful waiting after his article against Ernst Nolte had appeared, and about the friendly atmosphere of the conversations with Jacques Derrida at Northwestern University, unclouded by their earlier disputes. He sees it as his 'good fortune' that he 'met so many important Jewish scholars, in the US, in Israel and in Germany too'.

Sitting in the bus back to Gauting, I realize that, in that sentence, Habermas was taking stock. Since the 1950s, when he came into contact with the Institute for Social Research, he had taken the perspective of the Jewish survivors as an indispensable link to the unfinished project of German philosophy. Admittedly, the theory of communication and the theory of the modern society that he had developed as a German philosopher were independent of place and time: the norms of communication that he reconstructed are universal ones. The same can be said of the processes of rationalization that threaten – in all modern societies – to bring communicative action to a standstill in the iron cage of the system. But, at the same time, didn't Habermas continuously recall in his journalistic essays that German society is a special case, that it only found itself on the path of modernity via its moral catastrophe, and that the greatest danger it faces comes not from the side effects of modernization, but from the revival of a disastrous tradition whose ultimate logical consequence was revealed in Auschwitz? Was he not ceaselessly concerned, as a public intellectual, with the particular conditions under which universalism could be realized in this country? Hence the West German character of his cosmopolitan rationality; hence the contradictions between theory and practice; hence, ultimately, the need to confirm his own standpoint in dialogue with Jewish partners. Perhaps what constitutes Habermas's timeless legacy is precisely the point at which he was most inseparably linked to his time.

# Acknowledgements

I thank Arno Widmann for pointing out the 'Musketeers' of the Suhrkamp culture; Kristin Rotter for her wise battle plans; Christian Seeger for taking pleasure in the text; Oliver Kleppel and Stephen Roeper from the Archives Department of the Frankfurt am Main University Library for their friendly support; Martin Bauer, Andreas Bernard, David Höhn, Yael Reuveny and Tilman Spengler for their critical reading, valuable information and encouragement; and Jürgen Habermas for not putting any obstacles in the way of this book in spite of his scepticism.

# Notes

## An Afternoon in Starnberg

1 To keep the number of notes as small as possible, I have grouped several references in one note as follows: first the sources of the verbatim quotations and direct paraphrases, in the order of their occurrence in the text, then the references to further reading. Maak, 'Die absolute Form und die Geschichte', 102. On the Fruhtrunk painting, see Iden, 'Alles Linke auf seine Kappe'.

2 Habermas, 'Martin Heidegger: On the Publication of Lectures from the Year 1935', 161. On the preferences of the advocates of Critical Theory, see Bohrer, 'Sechs Szenen Achtundsechzig', 412. On the end of an era, see Müller-Doohm, *Habermas: A Biography*, 166–7. I have coined the term 'detached-house philosophy' after Andreas Koch's *'Einfamilienhaussoziologie'*.

3 Habermas, *The Past as Future*, 72.

4 Habermas, 'Modernity: An Incomplete Project', 14; Raulff, 'Akute Zeichen fiebriger Dekonstruktion'; Deleuze, 'Nomadic Thought', 259; Luhmann, *Social Systems*, 115, 114; Bolz, 'Niklas Luhmann und Jürgen Habermas', 34. On the French reaction to Habermas's affront, see Scholz, 'Innerdeutsches Frankreich', 66. The dinner with Foucault is mentioned in Eribon, *Michel Foucault et ses contemporains*, 291–2.

5 Jacob Taubes to Habermas, 15 January 1972, Papers of Jürgen Habermas, Archivzentrum, University Library, Goethe University, Frankfurt am Main (hereinafter UBA Ffm), Na 60, 18; Bohrer, '1968: Die Phantasie an die Macht?', 1073; Bohrer quoted in Müller-Doohm, *Habermas*, 493, n.90; Habermas, 'Vier Jungkonservative beim Projektleiter der Moderne'.

6 Michel, review of Habermas's *Theorie des kommunikativen Handelns*; Habermas, 'Philosophy as Stand-In and Interpreter', 20. On the discussion group with Fischer, see Habermas to Joschka Fischer, 12 February, 1986, UBA Ffm Na 60, 104.

7 Cusk, *Outline*, 16.

8 Axel Matthes to Habermas, 8 March 1979, UBA Ffm Na 60, 52; Dworkin quoted in Müller-Doohm, *Habermas*, 401. As early as 1980, the critic Peter Iden suspected that, among living philosophers, Habermas was the best-known outside the profession: Iden, 'Alles Linke auf seine Kappe'. On Habermas's international reception, see Corchia et al., *Habermas global*.

9 On the need for intellectual intuition, see Habermas, 'An Avantgardistic Instinct for Relevances', 55. Other quotations and paraphrases of Habermas are from our conversations at his home on 10 June 2022 and 1 September 2023.

10 The present book is not intended as a biography. As these notes indicate, it draws frequently on Stefan Müller-Doohm's indispensable *Habermas: A Biography*. Particularly instructive on the political and constitutional context of Habermas's thought is Specter, *Habermas: An Intellectual Biography*. On Habermas's early work, see Keulartz, *De verkeerde wereld van Jürgen Habermas*; Roman Yos, *Der junge Habermas*.

## In the Upside-Down World

1 Specter, *Habermas: An Intellectual Biography*, esp. 6–8, calls Habermas's generation the "58ers' to distinguish them explicitly from the "68ers'. Habermas's letter quoted in Müller-Doohm, *Habermas: A Biography*, 485, n.80. On Gaus's phrase – later made famous by Helmut Kohl – see 'Verschwiegene Enteignung:

Wer erfand die Wendung von der "Gnade der späten Geburt"?'. On the 1929 cohort, see, for example, Habermas, 'Die Liebe zur Freiheit'.

2 Illies, 'Jahrgang 1929'; Ypi, *Free: Coming of Age at the End of History*, 310.

3 Habermas, 'Ideologies and Society in the Post-war World', 43; Habermas, 'Political Experience and the Renewal of Marxist Theory', 79.

4 Habermas, *The Past as Future*, 48; Dahrendorf, 'Zeitgenosse Habermas', 480. On the motif of the missed opportunity, see, e.g., Habermas, 'Public Space and Political Public Sphere'.

5 Habermas, 'Im Lichte Heideggers'; 'Chemische Ferien vom Ich'; 'Philosophie ist Risiko'; 'Im Lichte Heideggers', translation after Müller-Doohm, *Habermas: A Biography*.

6 See Habermas, 'Das Absolute und die Geschichte'. See also Keulartz, *De verkeerde wereld van Jürgen Habermas*, 12–13, 47–8.

7 Habermas, 'Dialectics of Rationalization', 125–6. On the pairs of terms, see Keulartz, *De verkeerde wereld*, esp. 13, 24. Karl Heinz Bohrer also saw 'a kind of negative chiliasm' in Habermas's idea of constitutional patriotism: see Bohrer, 'Why We Are Not a Nation', 82.

8 Habermas, 'Martin Heidegger: On the Publication of Lectures from the Year 1935', 163, 164.

9 Jacob Taubes to Habermas, 28 January 1964, UBA Ffm Na 60, 5. On Habermas's relation to Heidegger, see Habermas, *The Philosophical Discourse of Modernity*, 136–7, 148ff. See also Habermas, '"Martin Heidegger? Nazi, sicher ein Nazi!"', 174; and Henrich, 'What Is Metaphysics?', 316.

10 Quoted in Hachmeister, *Heideggers Testament*, 59.

**Perpetrators and Victims**

1 Habermas quoted in Müller-Doohm, *Habermas: A Biography*, 74; Habermas, 'Vier Jungkonservative beim Projektleiter der Moderne'; Dahrendorf, 'Zeitgenosse Habermas', 478; Habermas

quoted in Müller-Doohm, *Habermas: A Biography*, 75. On Adorno's position as a spokesman, see Jureit and Schneider, *Gefühlte Opfer*, 107ff. Jacob Taubes mentions the atmosphere at the Institute for Social Research in a letter to Habermas dated 17 September 1969: 'You lived long enough in the orbit of the Frankfurt institute yourself – although in times when one's very existence was not endangered – to know that the lives of those who held subordinate posts there were not made easy' (UBA Ffm Na 60, 12). For a more thorough account of Habermas's start at the Institute, see Müller-Doohm, *Habermas: A Biography*, 73–80. On Scholem's impression, see Später, 'Der Verlorene: George Lichtheim findet ein offenes Ohr', 34. On Scholem's and Adorno's physiognomy of Benjamin, see Lorenz Jäger, *Walter Benjamin*, 66–7, 29.

2 Habermas, 'The German Idealism of the Jewish Philosophers', 21ff.; Habermas, 'Historical Consciousness and Post-Traditional Identity', 252.

3 Habermas, 'Gershom Scholem: The Torah in Disguise', 200. Cf. Scholem, 'Juden und Deutsche'. According to Christoph Schmidt (*Israel und die Geister von '68*, 74), Scholem's speech became a 'short catechism' for the Germans' relationship to the Jews.

4 Habermas, 'Gershom Scholem: The Torah in Disguise', 200–1.

5 Habermas, 'The German Idealism of the Jewish Philosophers', 41; Deutscher, *The Non-Jewish Jew and Other Essays*; Moses, *German Intellectuals and the Nazi Past*, Ch. 5. On the Jewish remigrants in East Germany, see *Ein anderes Land: Jüdisch in der DDR* ['Another country: Jewish in the GDR'], exhibition catalogue, Jewish Museum Berlin, 2023. On the role of the Frankfurt School as spokespersons, see Jureit and Schneider, *Gefühlte Opfer*, 107ff.

**Farewell to Profundity**

1 All quotations are from Habermas, 'Vorwort', in *Politik, Kunst, Religion*.

2 Habermas, 'Dialectics of Rationalization', 126, 97; see also 96ff.; Habermas, 'Vorwort zur Neuauflage 1990', 11; Habermas, *Also a History of Philosophy*, vol. 1, xvii. On the publishing success of the *Structural Transformation of the Public Sphere*, see Habermas, *A New Structural Transformation*, 1.

3 Habermas, 'Dialectics of Rationalization', 128–9; Honneth, 'Adorno und Habermas', 658.

4 Habermas, 'Dialectics of Rationalization', 128; Hans-Ulrich Wehler to Habermas, 24 January 1964, UBA Ffm Na 60, 4. Regina Schilling uses the term 'heart-attack generation' in her documentary *Kulenkampffs Schuhe* ['Kulenkampff's shoes'], Germany, 2018. On Wehler's track and field career, see Rahden, 'Die Gummersbacher Schule', 8.

5 Martin Bauer in conversation with the author. See Habermas, 'Ich bin alt, aber nicht fromm geworden', 197: 'My generation has taken leave of the formal tone and the pretense of German–Greek profundity.' Walser, *Leben und Schreiben*, 365. On Habermas and literary authors, see Cammann, 'Augenblicke der Liebe', 86–91.

6 Sloterdijk, in https://www.youtube.com/watch?v=zt9-3Qt2s1A; Habermas, 'Martin Heidegger: On the Publication of Lectures from the Year 1935', 155; 'Vorwort', in *Kleine Politische Schriften I–IV*, 9; 'Dialectics of Rationalization', 128–9. On the distinction between responsible and irresponsible minds, see Habermas, 'Dialectics of Rationalization', 127, and 'Why More Philosophy?', 637. On Enzensberger, see Habermas, *The Past as Future*, 16–17.

7 Bude, 'Die Soziologen der Bundesrepublik', 572; Habermas, 'Why More Philosophy?', 635; Jaeggi, 'Versöhnung als Puzzlearbeit'. On the necessity of distinguishing between theory and literature, see also Habermas, 'Philosophy and Science as Literature?', 205–27.

**The Consciousness of the Present**

1 Siegfried Kracauer to Karl Markus Michel, 15 August 1966, Siegfried Unseld Archive, *Theorie* series, German Literature

Archives, Marbach; Habermas, 'Dialectics of Rationalization', 99.

2  Taubes quoted in Felsch, *The Summer of Theory*, 43; Jacob Taubes to Habermas, 21 April 1964, UBA Ffm Na 60, 5; Habermas, 'Why More Philosophy?', 637, 639.

3  Habermas, 'The Classical Doctrine of Politics in Relation to Social Philosophy', 81; 'Knowledge and Human Interests: A General Perspective', 301; 'Vorwort', in *Politik, Kunst, Religion*, 7. Jacob Taubes mentions Habermas's tension in a letter to Habermas dated 25 January 1972, UBA Ffm Na 60, 18. On Husserl's asceticism, see Habermas, 'The German Idealism of the Jewish Philosophers', 30–1.

4  Michel quoted in Felsch, *The Summer of Theory*, 47; Hans Magnus Enzensberger to Habermas, 30 July 1965, UBA Ffm Na 60, 6.

5  Habermas, 'Über Titel, Texte und Termine', 48; Habermas, *The Structural Transformation of the Public Sphere*, 167. Cf. Enzensberger, 'Bildung als Konsumgut', 110–36.

6  Hofmann quoted in Müller-Doohm, *Habermas: A Biography*, 99; Adorno, *Minima Moralia*, 192.

7  Hans Paeschke to Habermas, 30 May 1968, UBA Ffm Na 60, 10. Frisch reproduced in facsimile in Bürger, 'Grüße vom Zaungast', 42.

8  Jacob Taubes to Habermas, 29 June 1965, UBA Ffm Na 60, 6; Habermas to Georg Ramseger, 22 January 1964, UBA Ffm Na 60, 4.

## The Center Does Not Hold

1  Habermas to Rolf Meyersohn, 29 January 1965, and Rolf Meyersohn to Habermas, 18 June 1965, both UBA Ffm Na 60, 6. The coinciding French colloquium is mentioned in a letter from Lucien Goldmann to Habermas, 18 October 1965: UBA Ffm Na 60, 6. Habermas's itinerary can be found in Müller-Doohm, *Habermas: A Biography*, 130. Habermas mentions television in America in 'Vorwort zur Neuauflage 1990', 29.

2  See Müller-Doohm, *Habermas: A Biography*, 143ff. On Enzensberger's sojourn in the US, see Enzensberger, *Tumult*, 2014, 134ff.

3  Habermas's letter is printed in facsimile in Müller-Doohm, *Habermas: A Biography*, illustration insert.

4  Didion, 'Slouching Towards Bethlehem', 84; Habermas to Peter L. Berger, 10 May 1967, UBA Ffm Na 60, 8; Habermas, 'Some Conditions for Revolutionizing Late Capitalist Societies', 40. On the changing attitudes towards Black domestic workers, see Tom Wolfe, 'Radical Chic'.

5  Warhol and Hackett, *POPism: The Warhol Sixties*, 16; on the year 1967, see pp. 253–4. The Handke episode is recounted in Müller-Doohm, *Habermas: A Biography*, 185.

6  Arno Widmann, 'Wahrheit und Gesellschaft'. On Habermas's return to Frankfurt, see Müller-Doohm, *Habermas: A Biography*, 145; on the significance of the United States, see p. 206; also see Iden, 'Alles Linke auf seine Kappe'.

## Running the Gauntlet in Frankfurt

1  Henrich, *Ins Denken ziehen*, 145; Fischer, 'Gründungsfigur des demokratischen Deutschland', 46; Habermas, 'Ein Brief', 393. On Habermas's sympathy for reformers, see Bohrer, *Jetzt*, 12–13.

2  Jacob Taubes to Robert Jauss, 26 May 1967, Estate of Jacob Taubes, Leibniz-Zentrum für Literatur- und Kulturforschung, Berlin. On the Hanover episode and its aftermath, see also Bohrer, '1968: Die Phantasie an die Macht?', 1073; Müller-Doohm, *Habermas: A Biography*, 141, and Witt-Stahl, 'Linksfaschismus', 43–45. Fried quoted in 'Linksfaschismus', 45.

3  All quotations are from Habermas, 'Die Scheinrevolution und ihre Kinder', 249–60.

4  Habermas, 'Knowledge and Human Interests', 314; Gerhard Stamer to Habermas, 28 October 1968, UBA Ffm Na 60, 10; Fischer, 'Gründungsfigur des demokratischen Deutschland', 47.

5  Negt quoted in Müller-Doohm, *Habermas: A Biography*, 100; Jaeggi, 'Versöhnung als Puzzlearbeit'.

6  Gehlen quoted in Habermas, 'Arnold Gehlen', 113; Marquard, *Schwierigkeiten mit der Geschichtsphilosophie*, 80; Habermas, 'Arnold Gehlen', 112; Bude, 'Die Soziologen der Bundesrepublik', 577; Habermas, 'Moral Universalism in a Time of Political Regression', 19–20. On Gehlen's retreat, see Müller-Doohm, *Habermas: A Biography*, 161.

7  Jacob Taubes, 'Memorandum für Siegfried Unseld', n.d., UBA Ffm Na 60, 10; Unseld, *Chronik 1970*, 29; for a chronology of the conflict, see pp. 22–96.

8  Peter Urban quoted in Müller-Doohm, *Habermas: A Biography*, 152. On the distinction between 'communicative' and 'strategic' action, see Habermas, 'Labour and Interaction', 151; Unseld's paraphrase in *Chronik*, 34.

9  Habermas quoted in Paul, *Suhrkamp Theorie*, 11. On Habermas's regret, see Unseld, *Chronik*, 70. On his subsequent standing, see Müller-Doohm, *Habermas: A Biography*, 153.

## Rocket Science for a Better Society

1  Strauss quoted in Dunkhase, 'Rückzug vom entzauberten Bewußtsein', 34. For the path from Marx to Hegel, see e.g. Habermas, 'Labour and Interaction'.

2  The 'weightiest of productive forces' in Habermas, 'Why More Philosophy?', 650; all other quotations are from *Knowledge and Human Interests*.

3  Enzensberger to Habermas, 30 July 1965, UBA Ffm Na 60, 6; Habermas to Enzensberger, 6 March 1967, and Enzensberger to Habermas, 13 March 1967, UBA Ffm Na 60, 8. On Habermas's lack of experience as an analysand, see Habermas, *Knowledge and Human Interests*, viii. On the Freud symposium, see Habermas, 'Psychischer Thermidor und die Wiedergeburt einer rebellischen Subjektivität', 321.

4  Habermas to Enzensberger, 17 March 1967, UBA Ffm Na 60, 8; Habermas, 'Die Scheinrevolution und ihre Kinder', 258. See also his critical characterization of Enzensberger quoted in Amslinger, *Verlagsautorschaft*, 390–1.

5 Habermas, *Knowledge and Human Interests*, 230; Habermas, 'A Philosophico-Political Profile', 163.

6 For Habermas's homage to Mitscherlich, see Habermas, *Knowledge and Human Interests*, viii. On *The Inability to Mourn* and that book's relationship to *Knowledge and Human Interests*, see Jureit and Schneider, *Gefühlte Opfer*, 124ff.

7 *Der Spiegel* and Marcuse quoted in Müller-Doohm, *Habermas: A Biography*, 166–7. On the students' accusations, see Heidemann, 'Die Verfolgung und Ermordung der Theorie durch die Praxis'. Max Pensky observes the parallelism of Habermas's and West Germany's 'life histories': see Pensky, 'Universalism and the Situated Critic', 69.

8 Habermas quoted in Wiggershaus, *Jürgen Habermas*, 102. See also Bude, 'Starnberg', 95.

9 Habermas, 'Why More Philosophy?', 643. On the Max Planck Institute in Starnberg, see Leendertz, 'Ungunst des Augenblicks', 105–16.

10 Habermas, 'History and Evolution', 10; Michael Redepenning (*Playboy*) quoted in Felsch, 'Das Bunny schaut nach links', 63. On Weizsäcker and futurology, see Seefried, *Shaping Tomorrow's World*, esp. 112ff. and 226ff.

11 Horowitz, 'Portrait of the Marxist as an Old Trouper'.

12 Habermas, 'The New Obscurity', 51; Horowitz, 'Portrait of the Marxist', 232. On the decline of future research, see Leendertz, 'Ungunst des Augenblicks'.

13 Dahrendorf quoting a self-description of Habermas's: Dahrendorf to Habermas, 3 November 1966, UBA Ffm Na 60, 7. Weizsäcker quoted in Müller-Doohm, *Habermas: A Biography*, 205 ('law and order' is in English in the original); Habermas quoted in Wiggershaus, *Jürgen Habermas*, 98. On Habermas as a boss, see Müller-Doohm, *Habermas: A Biography*, 177–8, 202–3.

**What We Must Presuppose**

1 Habermas attributes the term 'friendly living together' to Brecht in 'Dialectics of Rationalization', 125. The remaining quota-

tions are from Habermas, 'Vorbereitende Bemerkungen', 122, 137–8.

2 Habermas, 'Deliberative Democracy', 60; 'Knowledge and Human Interests', 314; 'Vorbereitende Bemerkungen', 140.

3 Spaemann, 'Die Utopie der Herrschaftsfreiheit', 735, 750.

4 Dahrendorf, 'Zeitgenosse Habermas', 482; Henrich, 'What Is Metaphysics', 315; Luhmann, 'Systemtheoretische Argumentationen', 332, 335. Foucault, 'The Ethics of the Concern for Self', 298. See also – supporting Luhmann – Norbert Bolz, 'Niklas Luhmann und Jürgen Habermas', 40: 'Ordinarily, one has no time for Habermasian discourse.'

5 Habermas quoted in Koller, 'Counterfactual Presuppositions', 520–1; Habermas, 'Truth and Society', 103.

6 Habermas, 'The New Obscurity', 69; Habermas, 'An Interview with Jurgen Habermas', 10; Habermas quoted in Koller, 'Counterfactual Presuppositions', 521; Habermas, The Past as Future, 102; Dahrendorf, 'Zeitgenosse Habermas', 484. In a 2020 interview, Habermas said, 'I am aware that I have not yet managed to convince the profession of this point' – i.e. of the assumption of a rationality inherent in our interactions: see 'Moral Universalism in a Time of Political Regression', 31. On the less concrete assumptions of communication theory, see Specter, Habermas: An Intellectual Biography, ch. 5.

7 Habermas, 'The Horizon of Modernity is Shifting', 4. See, e.g., Habermas, 'Dialectics of Rationalization', 115. Cf. Bude, 'Die Soziologen der Bundesrepublik', 577: 'The true object of his sociological observations are the weeklies, the journals of ideas and the discussion forums in which he keeps track of the thought motifs that are in the air.'

8 On West German discussion culture, see Nina Verheyen, Diskussionslust. See also Norbert Elias, Studies on the Germans. Kogon quoted in 'The Administered World, or: The Crisis of the Individual', interview with Adorno and Horkheimer, Hessischer Rundfunk, 4 September 1950, https://www.youtube.com/watch

?v=89o2VYn7MJc&t=85s. I am indebted to Lukas Rathjen for bringing this recording to my attention.

9  Habermas, 'Vier Jungkonservative beim Projektleiter'; Adorno, *Lectures on Negative Dialectics*, 57; Habermas, 'Dialectics of Rationalization', 99; Habermas, 'Why More Philosophy?', 641–2; Habermas, 'Apologetic Tendencies', 227.

## The Stigma of the Spoken

1  Habermas, 'Karl Jaspers über Schelling', 84. See Hannah Arendt, 'Truth and Politics', 49ff.
2  Habermas, 'Arnold Gehlen', 121.
3  Habermas, 'Dialectics of Rationalization', 126; Habermas, 'Public Space and Political Public Sphere', 12–13. 'Sentimentality towards persons' is accompanied by 'cynicism towards institutions', as we can read in *The Structural Transformation of the Public Sphere*, 172. In contrast to Hannah Arendt, Habermas, mistrustful towards charismatic representations, emphasized the private facets of the bourgeois public sphere in his theory; see *The Structural Transformation of the Public Sphere*, 11.
4  Habermas, 'Public Space and Political Public Sphere'. His disability had been 'not exactly a favourable condition in which to pursue a "career"', Habermas wrote to Martin Walser after Walser had painted a spiteful portrait of him as an enforcer of antifascist morals in the character of Professor Wesendonck in *Death of a Critic*, his 2002 *roman à clef*. Quoted in Müller-Doohm, *Habermas: A Biography*, 485.
5  Habermas, 'Public Space and Political Public Sphere'. The remark about paper is found in 'Dialectics of Rationalization', 129. Habermas to Udi Eichler, 16 April 1973, UBA Ffm Na 60, 19. On Habermas's predilection for writing as a student, see Müller-Doohm, *Habermas: A Biography*, 39. On the 'media intellectuals' – and on Habermas's early career in journalism – see Schildt, *Medien-Intellektuelle in der Bundesrepublik*.

6 Habermas, 'Public Space and Political Public Sphere'.

7 Habermas, *The Structural Transformation of the Public Sphere*, 163, cf. 170–1. Even today, Habermas emphasizes the importance of the 'democratic will-formation of *readers*' for the social integration of modern societies: see 'Moral Universalism at a Time of Political Regression', 32.

## Uncanny Germany

1 Habermas to Fritz Raddatz, 7 February 1977, UBA Ffm Na 60, 40.

2 On the West German 'repetition phobia', see Jureit and Schneider, *Gefühlte Opfer*, 124.

3 Habermas to Alexander Kluge, 21 March 1978, papers of Alexander Kluge, Akademie der Künste, Berlin.

4 Dregger and Sontheimer quoted in Habermas, 'Briefwechsel mit Kurt Sontheimer', 369–70; Habermas, 'Dialectics of Rationalization', 106; Habermas, 'A Test for Popular Justice', 368, 400, 384, 379, 400.

5 Habermas, 'Ich bin alt, aber nicht fromm geworden', 200–1; Ernst Nolte to Habermas, 17 March 1977, UBA Ffm Na 60, 40. The term '"civil war" of the '58ers' is used for example by Specter, *Habermas: An Intellectual Biography*, 8.

6 Habermas, 'Briefwechsel mit Kurt Sontheimer', 381–2; Habermas, 'Introduction', 17; Habermas, 'Political Experience and the Renewal of Marxist Theory', 82.

7 See Scherer, *Ungeheurer Alltag*.

8 See Alexander Kluge, '"Unheimlichkeit der Zeit"', 11.

## Theory of the Loss of Meaning

1 Habermas, 'Introduction', 10; Habermas, 'Political Experience and the Renewal of Marxist Theory', 89. On the need for urgency, see Habermas, 'Dialectics of Rationalization', 106. On the attempt to wrest the prerogative of interpretation from the conservatives, see Habermas, 'Modernity: An Incomplete Project', 7–8.

2 Habermas quoted in Amslinger, *Verlagsautorschaft*, 390ff.; Habermas, *The Theory of Communicative Action*, vol. 1, xlii; Habermas, 'Dialectics of Rationalization', 108, 104.

3 Habermas, 'Dialectics of Rationalization', 128.

4 Habermas, *The Theory of Communicative Action*, vols. 1 and 2, passim. For a concise presentation of the fundamental ideas, see Habermas, *The Philosophical Discourse of Modernity*, 350ff.

5 Habermas, 'The Dialectics of Rationalization', 113. The colonization thesis is developed in Habermas, *The Theory of Communicative Action*, vol. 2, Part VIII.

### Was That Really Necessary?

1 Rutschky, *Mitgeschrieben*, 122; Michel, review of Habermas's *Theorie des kommunikativen Handelns*. On the book's publication, see Müller-Doohm, *Habermas: A Biography*, 213. The print run is mentioned in Michel's review.

2 Bubner, 'Rationalität als Lebensform', 342; Busche, 'Sein oder Nichtsein'; Brunkhorst, 'Anteil der Moral an der Menschwerdung des Affen'.

3 Skinner, 'Habermas's Reformation', 38; Breuer, 'Die Depotenzierung der Kritischen Theorie', 132–146. For a Marxist perspective, see e.g. Habermas, 'Dialectics of Rationalization', 116ff.

4 Busche, 'Sein oder Nichtsein'.

5 Skinner, 'Habermas's Reformation', 38; Michel, review of Habermas's *Theorie des Kommunikativen Handelns*.

6 Busche, 'Sein oder Nichtsein'; Bubner, 'Rationalität als Lebensform', 343, 346; Arno Widmann in Habermas, 'Dialectics of Rationalization', 128.

7 Rutschky, *Mitgeschrieben*, 136; Ortheil, '"Königsweg der Individuation"', 241; Michel's review of Habermas's *Theorie des Kommunikativen Handelns*.

8 Jaeggi, 'Versöhnung als Puzzlearbeit'; Michel's review of Habermas's *Theorie des Kommunikativen Handelns*; Habermas,

'Modernity: An Incomplete Project', 13; Jaeggi, 'Versöhnung als Puzzlearbeit'.

9  'Scarce resources' are mentioned in, e.g., Habermas, *Theory of Communicative Action*, vol. 2, 227. On the similarity with left-alternative critiques of civilization, see Michel's review of Habermas's *Theorie des Kommunikativen Handelns*.

10  Strauss, *Couples, Passersby*, 69; Habermas, 'Introduction', 21; Michel, 'Der Grundwortschatz', 835 [not included in the English translation, *Observations on 'The Spiritual Situation of the Age'*].

11  Habermas to Cornelius Castoriadis, 7 July 1982, UBA Ffm Na 60, 73. Habermas's letter to Unseld quoted in Müller-Doohm, *Habermas: A Biography*, 196. On Habermas's withdrawal, see Paul, *Suhrkamp Theorie*, 256.

12  Habermas, 'Dialectics of Rationalization', 124; Habermas, 'Ideologies and Society in the Post-war World', 60. On the West German reception of Barthes's *Pleasure of the Text*, see e.g. Ortheil, 'Königsweg der Individuation', 241.

13  All quotations are from Habermas, 'Vier Jungkonservative beim Projektleiter'.

14  Rutschky, *Gegen Ende*, 258. On the theory of 'aesthetic-expressive' action, see Rutschky, 'Der Zwischenraum', 391. On the role of alcohol and cigarettes, see Rutschky, *Wartezeit*, 173ff.

## Taxonomy of the Counter-Enlightenment

1  Habermas, 'Mit dem Pfeil ins Herz der Gegenwart', 127 [The first sentence quoted is not present in the published English translation of this article]. Habermas, 'Taking Aim at the Heart of the Present', 175. On the 'broad present', see Gumbrecht, *Unsere breite Gegenwart*; Hartog, *Régimes d'historicité*.

2  See, e.g., Diez and Roth, *80*81*; Rödder, *21.0*; Bösch, *Zeitenwende 1979*; Sarasin, *1977*.

3  Habermas, 'Ein Brief', 394.

4  Habermas, 'Dialectics of Rationalization', 126; Habermas, 'Political Culture in Germany since 1968', 185; Habermas, 'Meine Jahre mit Helmut Kohl'.

5  Habermas, 'The New Obscurity', 50, 60; Habermas, 'Ein Interview mit der *New Left Review*', 257; Habermas, 'Political Culture in Germany since 1968', 192. Cf. Habermas, *The Past as Future*, 96–7.

6  Didion, 'Goodbye to All That', 225; Gadamer, 'Praise of Theory', 16.

7  Habermas, 'The Horizon of Modernity is Shifting', 9; Habermas, 'Modernity: An Incomplete Project', 9, 14.

8  Habermas, 'Briefwechsel mit Kurt Sontheimer', 381; Henrich, 'What Is Metaphysics', 309. On 'neo-' and 'post-', see Habermas, 'The Horizon of Modernity is Shifting', 3.

9  Habermas, 'Modernity: An Incomplete Project', 14; Habermas, 'Vier Jungkonservative beim Projektleiter'.

10  Jóhann Árnason to Habermas, 27 July 1971, UBA Ffm Na 60, 15.

11  Baier, *Französische Zustände*, 24. Some years later, Diedrich Diederichsen wrote analogously of German *Pop-Theorie*: 'In Germany, a song or the attitude of a band is received with ten times the intensity and twenty times the philosophy as (a) in its country of origin and (b) the song or the band merits' ('Deutschland 88: Wort auf!', 34). The rejection of Matthes's proposal is mentioned in Scholz, 'Innerdeutsches Frankreich', 66, whose interpretation informs this section and the next. On the French imports to West Germany, see Felsch, *The Summer of Theory*. On the fascination that Foucault emanated, see Bude, 'Starnberg', 99.

12  Gerd Bergfleth, 'Die zynische Aufklärung', 181, 188ff. On Rowohlt's *Literaturmagazin* and on Améry, see Felsch, *The Summer of Theory*, 94ff.

13  Habermas to Paul Veyne, 25 June 1981, UBA Ffm Na 60, 70; Paul Veyne quoted in Eribon, *Michel Foucault et ses contemporains*, 291. On the contrast Habermas drew between irony and earnest, see Miller, *The Passion of Michel Foucault*, 339. Miller's description of the meeting is more positive.

14  Foucault quoted in Eribon, *Michel Foucault et ses contemporains*, 292; Habermas to Michel Foucault, 23 August 1983, UBA

Ffm Na 60, 82. On the contrast between the 'universal' and the 'specific' intellectual, see e.g. Foucault, 'Truth and Power', 126–9.

## Distance and *Thymos*

1 Sloterdijk quoted in Müller-Doohm, *Habermas: A Biography*, 316. On the restricted objectives of Habermas's public engagement, see Pensky, 'Jürgen Habermas and the Antinomies of the Intellectual', 211–37.

2 Jaeggi, 'Versöhnung als Puzzlearbeit'; Habermas, 'Vorwort', in *Die Neue Unübersichtlichkeit*, 7. Christoph Möllers has observed that the use of rhetoric in Habermas's journalism is not justified by his theoretical writings: see 'Ach, Ästhetik!', 83ff. On Habermas's rhetorical 'side occupation', see Pensky, 'Jürgen Habermas and the Antinomies of the Intellectual', 216. I am indebted to Christian Marchlewitz for pointing out the concept of *Rollenprosa*, the fictional technique of a strongly characterized first-person narrator.

3 Habermas, 'Dialectics of Rationalization', 127. Habermas began even his 1953 critique of Heidegger with the words, 'We are concerned here with the philosopher Martin Heidegger not as a philosopher, but as a political personality, and with his influence not upon the internal discussion of scholars, but on the development of excitable and easily enthused students': Habermas, 'Martin Heidegger: On the Publication of Lectures from the Year 1935', 155.

4 Habermas, *The Philosophical Discourse of Modernity*, 336–7.

5 Habermas, 'Dialectics of Rationalization', 127. On the lack of consistency between his roles, see also Möllers, 'Ach, Ästhetik!', 83ff.

6 Habermas, 'Political Experience and the Renewal of Marxist Theory', 83; Jaeggi, 'Versöhnung als Puzzlearbeit'.

## J'accuse

1 The phrase that Habermas 'started and won' the *Historikerstreit* is from Peter Glotz, quoted in Lau, 'Öffentlichkeit und Beharrung';

Habermas, 'Heinrich Heine and the Role of the Intellectual in Germany', 95–6, 73.

2  Nolte, 'Vergangenheit, die nicht vergehen will'; Nolte quoted in Pokatzky, 'Saul Friedländer: Pavel, Paul, Shaul'.

3  See e.g. Sprügel, 'Der Katechet des Unsinns'; Habermas, 'Apologetic Tendencies', 227. There, Habermas mentions a 'NATO philosophy'; the expression was soon extended by others to 'NATO historians'; see e.g. Nipperdey, 'Wozu Geschichte gut ist', 7. The quotation about the 'break in continuity' is from a later text: Habermas, 'Yet Again: German Identity', 227.

4  For an excellent survey, see Herbert, 'Der Historikerstreit', 94–113. See also the foreword by René Schlott and the afterword by Christian Seeger in Hilberg, *Die Vernichtung der europäischen Juden*.

5  Herbert, 'Der Historikerstreit', 105–6; Habermas, 'Political Culture in Germany since 1968', 194; Habermas, 'Ich bin alt, aber nicht fromm', 204. On the end of the dispute, see e.g. Neiman, 'Wie die beiden Historikerstreite zusammenhängen', 7. For Nolte's television appearances, see the documentary by Andreas Christoph Schmidt, *Ernst Nolte – ein deutscher Streitfall*, Germany 2013.

6  Moses, 'Der Katechismus der Deutschen'; Omri Boehm, 'Macht den Mund auf!'. See also the contributions in Neiman and Wildt, *Historiker streiten*.

7  Habermas et al., 'Principles of Solidarity'. For a critical position, see e.g. 'The Principle of Human Dignity Must Apply to All People', *Guardian*, 22 November 2023. The problem of uniting German commemorative politics with a multicultural society was raised by Pensky, 'Jürgen Habermas and the Antinomies of the Intellectual', 230. See also Leo, *Tränen ohne Trauer*.

8  Ernst Tugendhat to Habermas, 12 July 1986, UBA Ffm Na 60, 109.

9  Habermas, 'Statt eines Vorworts'. See also Michael Wildt's critical review: *Verbrechen ohne Namen*.

10  Wolfgang Mommsen to Habermas, 18 November 1986, UBA
    Ffm Na 60, 106; Hans-Ulrich Wehler to Habermas, 1 September
    1986, UBA Ffm Na 60, 109; Martin Broszat to Habermas,
    8 October 1986, UBA Ffm Na 60, 102. On the situation of the
    historical discipline in Germany in the early 1980s, see Maier,
    *The Unmasterable Past*, 38f.

11  Hildebrand, 'Das Zeitalter der Tyrannen', 86; Nipperdey, 'Unter
    der Herrschaft des Verdachts', 218; Geiss, *Die Habermas-
    Kontroverse*, 176; Habermas, 'On the Public Use of History', 168.
    On the inference that the *Historikerstreit* was a continuation of
    Habermas's battle against supposed enemies of modernity, see
    also Maier, *The Unmasterable Past*, 40.

12  Habermas, 'The New Obscurity', 61.

13  Habermas, 'The New Intimacy between Culture and Politics',
    197 [translation modified]; Türcke, 'Darüber schweigen sie
    alle', 770; Herbert, 'Der Historikerstreit', 97. On the social
    paradigm shift on culture, see Kaube, 'Geschichtspatriotismus',
    120.

14  Jürgen Habermas, 'Keine Normalisierung der Vergangenheit',
    13.

**Back from the Future**

 1  Habermas, 'Martin Heidegger: On the Publication of Lectures
    from the Year 1935', 163; Habermas, 'Über den moralischen
    Notstand in der Bundesrepublik', 96, 98; Frei, 'Deutsche
    Vergangenheit und postkoloniale Katechese', 42. According to
    Müller-Doohm (*Habermas: A Biography*, 130), Habermas did
    not teach any class 'on the problem of "fascism"' during his first
    professorship in Frankfurt in the 1960s.

 2  West Germany is called 'purely a future project' by Geulen,
    'Bundesrepublikanismus', 22; Lübbe, 'Der Nationalsozialismus
    im deutschen Nachkriegsbewusstsein'; the 'avoidance of the con-
    crete' is from Herbert, 'Der Historikerstreit', 101. On Habermas,
    see Widmann, 'Wahrheit und Gesellschaft'; on the '68 genera-
    tion, see Schmidt, *Israel und die Geister von '68*.

3 Koselleck, 'Wozu noch Historie?', 1, 14; Mommsen, *Die Geschichtswissenschaft jenseits des Historismus*, 41, 27. On the importance of the Fischer controversy and the paradigm shift in the West German study of history, see Evans, *In Hitler's Shadow*, 113–14.

4 Habermas, 'History and Evolution', 8, 39–40. On the limited theoretical horizons of the Bielefeld School of social history, see Habermas, *The Theory of Communicative Action*, vol. 2, 376.

5 Habermas, 'Können komplexe Gesellschaften eine vernünftige Identität ausbilden?'.

6 Gustav Seibt, 'Die Formen der Historie', 903; Mommsen, *Die Geschichtswissenschaft jenseits des Historismus*, 30. For a good overview, see Esposito, *Zeitenwandel*.

7 Mann, 'The Old History and the New', 17. For Habermas's assessment, see *Kollektive Erinnerungsprozesse in Beziehung zur NS-Zeit*.

8 Schmid quoted in Fetscher, 'Die Suche nach der nationalen Identität', 121. Bohrer, 'Deutschland – noch eine geistige Möglichkeit'.

9 Walser, *Leben und Schreiben: Tagebücher 1974–1978*, 423; Walser, *Schreiben und Leben: Tagebücher 1979–1981*, 51; Walser, 'Handshake with Ghosts', 45, 47, 42.

10 Walser, *Tagebücher 1979–1981*, 229–30.

11 Walser, *Schreiben und Leben: Tagebücher 1979–1981*, 226–30. For Habermas's view of the evening, see Habermas, 'Begegnungen mit Gershom Scholem', 9.

12 Walser, 'Handshake with Ghosts', 42; Scholem, 'Address'; Walser, 'Experiences on Composing a Sunday Speech', 89–90.

13 Dahrendorf, 'Zur politischen Kultur der Bundesrepublik', 71; von Weizsäcker, 'Speech during the Ceremony Commemorating the 40th Anniversary of the End of War in Europe'. The present interpretation of Weizsäcker's speech paraphrases Dirk Moses, 'Deutschlands Erinnerungskultur und der "Terror der Geschichte"', 226.

14 Wiesel quoted in Herbert, 'Der Historikerstreit', 97; Habermas, 'Keine Normalisierung der Vergangenheit', 11–12. Part of *Die neue Unübersichtlichkeit*, including the title essay 'The New Obscurity', is found in English translation in the collection *The New Conservatism*.

**History and Memory**

1 Saul Friedländer to Habermas, 26 November 1985, UBA Ffm Na 60, 104. On the colloquium at the *Wissenschaftskolleg*, see Friedländer, *Where Memory Leads*, 213ff., and the transcript of the event itself, *Kollektive Erinnerungsprozesse in Beziehung zur NS-Zeit*.

2 On the Stuttgart conference, see Brechtken, 'Raul Hilberg, der Begriff Holocaust', 63ff.

3 This quotation and those that follow are from *Kollektive Erinnerungsprozesse in Beziehung zur NS-Zeit*.

4 On Wapnewski's party membership, cf. https://www.deutschlandfunk.de/die-geister-die-man-rief-100.html.

5 Habermas to Saul Friedländer, 7 April 1986, UBA Ffm Na 60, 104. The Berlin episodes are described in Pokatzky, 'Saul Friedländer: Pavel, Paul, Shaul', and Friedländer, *Where Memory Leads*, 209ff.

**Stirrings of Post-National Feeling**

1 Habermas, 'Yet Again: German Identity', 85; Winkler quoted in *Kollektive Erinnerungsprozesse in Beziehung zur NS-Zeit*. On Habermas's hesitation, see the introduction to Part 6 of his essay collection *Die nachholende Revolution*, 177; on his earlier attitude towards German unity, see Habermas, *The Past as Future*, 48–9.

2 Habermas quoted in Rauh, *Philosophie aus einer abgeschlossenen Welt*, 53. For the recapitulation of his relationship to the GDR, see Habermas, *The Past as Future*, 34–5. Biermann quoted in an email of 19 November 2023. I am grateful to Ralf Eichberg of Naumburg for a description of the crowded lecture hall.

Andreas Maercker to Habermas, 15 January 1986, and Habermas to Andreas Maercker, 16 April 1986, both UBA Ffm Na 60, 106. Maercker mentions Habermas's book shipment in a text on his website: 'Politisch-philosophische Exzerpte eines jungen Ostdeutschen um 1980' ['Political-philosophical fragments by a young East German circa 1980'], http://www.maercker-web site.ch/images/data/Polit_phil_Exzerpte_jungen_Mannes_150 508.pdf, 2.

3 Habermas, *The Past as Future*, 35–6.
4 Bohrer, *Jetzt*, 287. Bohrer's autobiography, in which Habermas is prominent as 'the philosopher', also describes their friendship.
5 Habermas, 'Introduction', 24; Karl Heinz Bohrer to Habermas, 12 July 1986, UBA Ffm Na 60, 102. Bohrer's series on West Germany, 'Die Unschuld an die Macht! Eine politische Typologie' consisted of three articles with titles of their own: 'Die Schaden vom Volke wenden', 'Die Zombies' and 'Die guten Hirten'. See also Bohrer's earlier 'Die Ästhetik des Staates'.
6 Bohrer, 'Why We Are Not a Nation', 73. The description of Habermas's sixtieth birthday celebration and Bohrer's surprising choice draws on *Jetzt*, 301–2, 315–16.
7 Bohrer, 'Why We Are Not a Nation', 74, 79, 76. On Habermas's Frankfurt speech, see Bohrer, *Jetzt*, 12.
8 Bohrer, 'Why We Are Not a Nation', 82; Habermas, 'Yet Again: German Identity', 98; Bohrer, 'Die Ästhetik des Staates revisited', 750; Seibt, 'Zyklus von Erniedrigung und Überhebung', 334.
9 Habermas, 'Political Culture in Germany since 1968', 184; Habermas, 'Die Stunde der nationalen Empfindung', 163; Reemtsma, 'Erinnerung vergemeinschaften', 30; Habermas, 'Why More Philosophy?', 642. For Habermas's defence of late West Germany, see e.g. *The Past as Future*, 57. On the spread of post-national mentality, see Habermas, 'Yet Again: German Identity', 86–7. On the rise of *Politikverdrossenheit*, disillusionment with politics, cf. Ulrich Herbert, *A History of Twentieth-century Germany*, 804.
10 Bohrer, *Jetzt*, 316; Karl Heinz Bohrer to Habermas, 30 December

1989; 1, 2 and 29 May 1990, and Habermas to Karl Heinz Bohrer, 15 October 1990, all UBA Ffm Na 60, 143.

11 Habermas, 'Yet Again: German Identity', 96; Habermas, *The Past as Future*, 43–4; Habermas, 'What Does Socialism Mean Today?', 5. On the significance of the German reunification for Habermas's theory, see Specter, *Habermas: An Intellectual Biography*, ch. 5. See also Hacke, 'Wir-Gefühle', 12–32.

12 Habermas quoted in Wolf, *Parting from Phantoms*, 115, 111; Habermas, *The Past as Future*, 37.

13 Wolf, *Parting from Phantoms*, 120; Dieckmann, 'Weder Wunsch- noch Schreckvorstellung', 337–8. See also Dieckmann, 'Die Deutschen und die Nation', 656.

14 Habermas, 'Die Stunde der nationalen Empfindung', 163. Cf. Habermas, '1989 in the Shadow of 1945'. For the thesis of the collective injury of the Eastern Europeans, see Krastev and Holmes, *The Light that Failed*.

**The Primacy of Global Domestic Politics**

1 Habermas, 'Political Experience and the Renewal of Marxist Theory', 88. On the young Habermas's attitude towards Europe, see Müller-Doohm, *Habermas: A Biography*, 356–7. On the limitations of Habermas's diagnosis of the times, see Kaube, 'Die geistige Situation der Zeit'.

2 Habermas, 'An Avantgardistic Instinct for Relevances', 56; 'An Interview with Jurgen Habermas', 16.

3 Habermas, 'Is the Development of a European Identity Necessary?', 81; Habermas, *The Crisis of the European Union*, 116–17.

4 Hans-Georg Gadamer to Habermas, 14 August 1972, UBA Ffm Na 60, 16; Habermas, 'Historical Consciousness and Post-Traditional Identity', 251.

5 On the reflexive nature of collective identity formation, see e. g. Habermas, 'Does Europe Need a Constitution?', 100–1.

6 Jan Philipp Reemtsma, 'Auf den Friedenspreisträger 2001';

170 Notes to pp. 133–138

Habermas, *The Past as Future*, 46; Habermas, *Between Facts and Norms*, xliii.

7 Habermas, 'An Avantgardistic Instinct for Relevances', 56; Habermas, *The Crisis of the European Union*, 2; Habermas, 'Citizenship and National Identity', 507; Habermas, 'Is the Development of a European Identity Necessary?', 81; Anderson, 'After the Event', 52. On the unanimity of the West in the Ukraine war, see also Neumann, 'Seine Sorge'.

8 Otfried Höffe quoted in Habermas, *Between Facts and Norms*, xl, n.5; Habermas, 'Schlusswort', 37; 'Habermas als Popstar'; Jan Ross, 'Hegel der Bundesrepublik'. On Habermas's relationship with Fischer, see Habermas to Joschka Fischer, 12 February 1986, UBA Ffm Na 60, 104, and Fischer, 'Gründungsfigur des demokratischen Deutschland', 49. On the Greens in general, see Habermas, *The Past as Future*, 90–1.

9 Olaf Scholz, 'Ab und an lese ich auch Comics'.

**On War**

1 Habermas, 'War and Indignation'. Cf. Habermas, 'A Plea for Negotiations'.

2 Snyder, 'Jürgen Habermas and Ukraine'; Krause, 'Eskalationsphobie'; Strauss, 'Hart verteidigte Illusionen'; Melnyk quoted in 'Habermas plädiert für schnelle Verhandlungen'; Geyer, 'Habermas'. On 'national pacifism': I have not seen the neologism *Nationalpazifismus* in print, but I first heard it during the debate on Habermas's first Ukraine article.

3 Habermas, 'Political Experience and the Renewal of Marxist Theory', 79; Habermas, *The Past as Future*, 16–17 (the comment on Enzensberger), 27; Habermas, 'Wider die Logik des Krieges'; Habermas, 'War and Indignation'. Habermas's defence of civil disobedience is found in 'Ziviler Ungehorsam'. For a summary of Habermas's position on military interventions, see Müller-Doohm, *Habermas: A Biography*, 279–88.

4 Letter quoted in Müller-Doohm, *Habermas: A Biography*, 281.

Habermas, 'Bestiality and Humanity'. The lack of a 'police force': *The Past as Future*, 12.

5 Habermas, 'Bestiality and Humanity'; for 'global domestic policy', see Habermas, *The Past as Future*, 22.

6 Merkel and Simon quoted in Müller-Doohm, *Habermas: A Biography*, 283–4; Handke quoted in Blanke, 'Recht und Moral im Kosovo-Krieg', 412.

7 Habermas, 'Interpreting the Fall of a Monument', 704, 703.

8 Habermas, 'Fundamentalism and Terror', 3.

9 Habermas, 'February 15, or What Binds Europeans', 40; Habermas, 'Interpreting the Fall of a Monument'; Habermas, 'Core Europe as Counterpower?', 50.

10 Habermas, 'An Interview on War and Peace', 110.

11 Habermas, 'A Plea for Negotiations'; Habermas, 'Bestiality and Humanity'; Habermas: 'Europe's Mistake'.

12 Habermas, 'Europe's Mistake', 182; Strauss quoted in Bluhm, 'Ein politischer Denkzettel aus Chicago', 29.

**The Philosopher of the Universal Provinces**

1 Goetz, 'Absoluter Idealismus: Bericht', 12; Boris Pistorius quoted in the German public broadcasting network ZDF: 'Reicht das, was Pistorius macht? "Nein"', interview with Sönke Neitzel, https://www.zdf.de/nachrichten/politik/neitzel-zeitenwende -pistorius-interview-berlin-direkt-100.html.

2 The 'collapse of the American party system': see Habermas, 'Europe's Mistake', 185. Habermas used a similar expression in our conversation. On the decline of the West, see most recently Rudolph, 'Tocqueville global'.

3 On Europe's 'globally inflential role', 'yesterday's news' and the defence of 'idealism', see Habermas, 'Europe's Mistake', 182, 185.

# References

Theodor W. Adorno, *Lectures on Negative Dialectics: Fragments of a Lecture Course, 1965/1966*, Cambridge 2008.

Theodor W. Adorno, *Minima Moralia: Reflections from Damaged Life*, trans. E. F. N. Jephcott, London 1978.

Tobias Amslinger, *Verlagsautorschaft: Enzensberger und Suhrkamp*, Göttingen, 2018.

Perry Anderson, 'After the Event', in *New Left Review*, 73 (2012), 49–61.

Hannah Arendt, 'Truth and Politics', in *The New Yorker*, 25 February 1967, 49ff.

Lothar Baier, *Französische Zustände: Berichte und Essays* ['French conditions: Reports and essays'], Frankfurt am Main 1982.

Gerd Bergfleth, 'Die zynische Aufklärung' ['The cynical Enlightenment'], in Bergfleth et al., *Zur Kritik der palavernden Aufklärung* ['Criticizing the babbling Enlightenment'], Munich 1984, 180–97.

Thomas Blanke, 'Recht und Moral im Kosovo-Krieg: Eine Auseinandersetzung mit Jürgen Habermas' ['Law and morality in the Kosovo war: A debate with Jürgen Habermas'], in *Kritische Justiz*, 32, no. 3 (1999), 410–25.

Harald Bluhm, 'Ein politischer Denkzettel aus Chicago: Leo Strauss liest die Leviten' ['A political warning from Chicago: Leo Strauss teaches a lesson'], in *Zeitschrift für Ideengeschichte*, 15, no. 3 (2021), 28–30.

Omri Boehm, 'Macht den Mund auf! Deutschland braucht eine mündigere öffentliche Diskussion über Israel – im Geiste der Aufklärung' ['Speak up! Germany needs a more responsible public discussion on Israel: In the spirit of the Enlightenment'], in *Die Zeit*, 21 October 2015.

Karl Heinz Bohrer, '1968: Die Phantasie an die Macht? Studentenbewegung – Walter Benjamin – Surrealismus' ['1968: Power to the imagination? Student movement; Walter Benjamin; Surrealism'], in *Merkur*, 585 (1997), 1069–80.

Karl Heinz Bohrer, 'Die Ästhetik des Staates' ['The aesthetics of the state'], in *Merkur*, 423 (1984), 1–15.

Karl Heinz Bohrer, 'Die Ästhetik des Staates revisited' ['The aesthetics of the state revisited'], in *Merkur*, 689/90 (2006), 749–57.

Karl Heinz Bohrer, 'Deutschland – noch eine geistige Möglichkeit: Bemerkungen zu einem nationalen Tabu' ['Germany: Still a spiritual possibility; remarks on a national taboo'], in *Frankfurter Allgemeine Zeitung*, 28 April 1979.

Karl Heinz Bohrer, *Jetzt: Geschichte meines Abenteuers mit der Phantasie* ['Now: Story of my adventure with imagination'], Frankfurt am Main 2017.

Karl Heinz Bohrer, 'Sechs Szenen Achtundsechzig' ['Six scenes of sixty-eight'], in *Merkur*, 708 (2008), 410–24.

Karl Heinz Bohrer, 'Die Unschuld an die Macht! Eine politische Typologie' ['Power to innocence! A political typology']. Part 1: 'Die Schaden vom Volke wenden' ['To deflect harm from the nation'], in *Merkur*, 425 (1984), 342–6.

Karl Heinz Bohrer, 'Die Unschuld an die Macht!' Part 2: 'Die Zombies' ['The zombies'], in *Merkur*, 427 (1984), 587–91.

Karl Heinz Bohrer, 'Die Unschuld an die Macht!' Part 3: 'Die guten Hirten' ['The good shepherds'], in *Merkur*, 431 (1985), 74–8.

Karl Heinz Bohrer, 'Why We Are Not a Nation – And Why We Should Become One', in *New German Critique*, 52 (Winter 1991), 72–83.

Norbert Bolz, 'Niklas Luhmann und Jürgen Habermas: Eine Phantomdebatte' ['Niklas Luhmann and Jürgen Habermas: A phantom debate'], in Wolfram Burckhardt (ed.), *Luhmann Lektüren* ['Luhmann readings'], Berlin 2010, 34–52.

Frank Bösch, *Zeitenwende 1979: Als die Welt von heute began* ['Watershed 1979: When the world of today began'], Munich 2019.

Magnus Brechtken, 'Raul Hilberg, der Begriff Holocaust und die Konferenzen von San José bis Stuttgart' ['Raul Hilberg, the term "Holocaust" and the conferences from San José to Stuttgart'], in René Schlott (ed.), *Raul Hilberg und die Holocaust-Historiographie*, Göttingen 2019, 47–70.

Stefan Breuer, 'Die Depotenzierung der Kritischen Theorie: Über Jürgen Habermas' "Theorie des kommunikativen Handelns"' ['The disempowerment of Critical Theory: On Jürgen Habermas's *Theory of Communicative Action*'], in *Leviathan*, 10, no. 1 (1982), 132–46.

Hauke Brunkhorst, 'Anteil der Moral an der Menschwerdung des Affen: Jürgen Habermas' Theorie des kommunikativen Handelns' ['Morality's part in the evolution from apes to humans: Jürgen Habermas's *Theory of Communicative Action*'], in *Frankfurter Rundschau*, 13 March 1982.

Rüdiger Bubner, 'Rationalität als Lebensform: Zu Jürgen Habermas' "Theorie des kommunikativen Handelns"' ['Rationality as a form of life: On Jürgen Habermas's *Theory of Communicative Action*'], in *Merkur*, 406 (1982), 341–55.

Heinz Bude, 'Die Soziologen der Bundesrepublik' ['The sociologists of West Germany'], in *Merkur*, 520 (1992), 569–80.

Heinz Bude, 'Starnberg', in *Zeitschrift für Ideengeschichte*, 15, no. 3 (2021), 92–9.

Jan Bürger, 'Grüße vom Zaungast: Max Frisch nähert sich im Schatten der Revolte' ['Greetings from an uninvited guest:

Max Frisch approaches in the shadow of rebellion'], in *Zeitschrift für Ideengeschichte*, 15, no. 3 (2021), 40–3.

Jürgen Busche, 'Sein oder Nichtsein das ist nicht die Frage; Jürgen Habermas und seine "Theorie des kommunikativen Handelns"' ['To be or not to be: That is not the question; Jürgen Habermas and his *Theory of Communicative Action*'], in *Frankfurter Allgemeine Zeitung*, 27 February 1982.

Alexander Cammann, 'Augenblicke der Liebe: Der Philosoph und die Literaten' ['Moments of love: The philosopher and the literary authors'], in *Zeitschrift für Ideengeschichte*, 15, no. 3 (2021), 86–91.

Lucia Corchia et al. (eds.), *Habermas global: Wirkungsgeschichte eines Werks* ['Habermas globally: The reception history of an *œuvre*'], Frankfurt am Main 2019.

Rachel Cusk, *Outline*, London 2018.

Ralf Dahrendorf, 'Zur politischen Kultur der Bundesrepublik' ['On the political culture of West Germany'], in *Merkur*, 455 (1987), 68–72.

Ralf Dahrendorf, 'Zeitgenosse Habermas: Jürgen Habermas zum sechzigsten Geburtstag' ['Our contemporary Habermas: For Jürgen Habermas on his sixtieth birthday'], in *Merkur*, 484 (1989), 478–87.

Gilles Deleuze, 'Nomadic Thought', in *Desert Islands and Other Texts 1953–1974*, Los Angeles 2004, 252–61.

Isaac Deutscher, *The Non-Jewish Jew and Other Essays*, London 2018.

Joan Didion, 'Goodbye to All That', in *Slouching Towards Bethlehem: Essays*, New York 2008, 225–38.

Joan Didion, 'Slouching Towards Bethlehem', in *Slouching Towards Bethlehem: Essays*, New York 2008, 84–128.

Friedrich Dieckmann, 'Die Deutschen und die Nation' ['The Germans and the nation'], in *Merkur*, 509 (1991), 649–59.

Friedrich Dieckmann, 'Weder Wunsch- noch Schreckvorstellung: Zur Frage der deutschen Staatseinheit' ['Neither a wishful nor fearful thinking: On the question of the unity of the German state'], in *Merkur*, 494 (1990), 335–40.

Diedrich Diederichsen, 'Deutschland 88: Wort auf!' ['Germany 88: [on lyrics]'], in *Spex*, 1988, 9, 34–5.

Georg Diez and Christopher Roth, *80\*81*, 11 vols., Zurich 2011.

Jan Eike Dunkhase, 'Rückzug vom entzauberten Bewußtsein Karl Löwith fragte nach der Natur der Dinge' ['Retreat from enchanted consciousness: Asked about the nature of things'], in *Zeitschrift für Ideengeschichte*, 15, no. 3 (2021), 30–4.

Norbert Elias, *Studies on the Germans*, Dublin 2013.

Hans Magnus Enzensberger, 'Bildung als Konsumgut: Analyse der Taschenbuch-Produktion', in *Einzelheiten* ['Culture as a consumer good: Analysis of paperback production'], Frankfurt am Main 1962, 110–36.

Hans Magnus Enzensberger, *Tumult*, Berlin 2014.

Didier Eribon, *Michel Foucault et ses contemporains* ['Michel Foucault and his contemporaries'], Paris 1994.

Fernando Esposito (ed.), *Zeitenwandel: Transformationen geschichtlicher Zeitlichkeit nach dem Boom Boom* ['Changing times: Transformations of historical temporality after the boom'], Göttingen 2017.

Richard J. Evans, *In Hitler's Shadow: West German Historians and the Attempt to Escape from the Nazi Past*, New York 1989.

Philipp Felsch, 'Das Bunny schaut nach links' ['The bunny faces left'], in *Zeitschrift für Ideengeschichte*, 15, no. 3 (2021), 61–3.

Philipp Felsch, *The Summer of Theory: History of a Rebellion, 1960–1990*, Cambridge 2022.

Iring Fetscher, 'Die Suche nach der nationalen Identität' ['The search for national identity'], in Jürgen Habermas (ed.), *Stichworte zur "Geistigen Situation der Zeit"* ['Keywords on the "spiritual situation of the time"'], vol. 1: *Nation und Republik*, Frankfurt am Main 1979, 115–31.

Joschka Fischer, 'Gründungsfigur des demokratischen Deutschland' ['Founding figure of democratic Germany'], in Michael Funken (ed.), *Über Habermas: Gespräche mit Zeitgenossen*, Darmstadt 2008, 45–57.

Michel Foucault, 'The Ethics of the Concern for Self as a Practice of Freedom', in *Ethics, Subjectivity and Truth*, New York 1997.

Michel Foucault, 'Truth and Power', in James D. Faubion (ed.), *Power: The Essential Works of Michel Foucault 1954–1984*, London 2019, 111–53.

Norbert Frei, 'Deutsche Vergangenheit und postkoloniale Katechese' ['Germany's past and postcolonial catechesis'], in Saul Friedländer et al., *Verbrechen ohne Namen: Anmerkungen zum neuen Streit über den Holocaust*, Munich 2022, 33–51.

Saul Friedländer, *Where Memory Leads: My Life*, New York 2016.

Hans-Georg Gadamer, 'Praise of Theory', in *Praise of Theory: Speeches and Essays*, trans. Chris Dawson, New Haven 1998, 16–36.

Imanuel Geiss, *Die Habermas-Kontroverse: Ein deutscher Streit* ['The Habermas controversy: A German dispute'], Berlin 1988.

Christian Geulen, 'Bundesrepublikanismus: Überlegungen zur Vorgeschichte der Gegenwart' ['Federal republicanism: Thoughts on the prehistory of the present'], in *Merkur*, 893 (2023), 19–33.

Christian Geyer, 'Habermas', in *Frankfurter Allgemeine Zeitung*, 16 February 2023.

Rainald Goetz, 'Absoluter Idealismus: Bericht' ['Absolute idealism: A report'], in *Zeitschrift für Ideengeschichte*, 17, no. 1 (2023), 5–16.

Hans Ulrich Gumbrecht, *Unsere breite Gegenwart* ['Our broad present'], Frankfurt am Main 2016.

Jürgen Habermas, '1989 in the Shadow of 1945: On the Normality of a Future Berlin Republic', in *A Berlin Republic: Writings on Germany*, trans. Steven Rendall, Lincoln, NE 1997, 161–81.

Jürgen Habermas, 'Das Absolute und die Geschichte: Von der Zwiespältigkeit in Schellings Denken' ['The absolute and history: on the ambivalence in Schelling's thought'], unpublished inaugural lecture, Bonn 1954.

Jürgen Habermas, *Also a History of Philosophy*, vol. 1: *The Project of a Genealogy of Postmetaphysical Thinking*, trans. Ciaran Cronin, Cambridge 2023.

Jürgen Habermas, 'Apologetic Tendencies', in *The New Conservatism: Cultural Criticism and the Historians' Debate*, trans. Shierry Weber Nicholsen, Cambridge, MA 1991, 212–28.

Jürgen Habermas, 'Arnold Gehlen: Imitation Substantiality', in *Philosophical-Political Profiles*, Frankfurt am Main 1987, 111–28.

Jürgen Habermas, 'An Avantgardistic Instinct for Relevances: The Role of the Intellectual and the European Cause', in *Europe: The Faltering Project*, trans. Ciaran Cronin, Cambridge 2009, 49–58.

Jürgen Habermas, 'Begegnungen mit Gershom Scholem' ['An encounter with Gershom Scholem], in *Münchner Beiträge zur jüdischen Geschichte und Kultur*, 2 (2007), 9–18.

Jürgen Habermas, 'Bestiality and Humanity: A War on the Border between Legality and Morality', trans. Stephen Meyer and William E. Scheurman, in *Constellations*, 6, no. 3 (1999), 263–72.

Jürgen Habermas, *Between Facts and Norms: Contributions to a Discourse Theory of Law and Democracy*, trans. William Rehg, Cambridge, MA 1996.

Jürgen Habermas, 'Ein Brief' ['A letter'], in Rainer Erd et al. (eds.), *Kritische Theorie und Kultur* ['Critical Theory and culture'], Frankfurt am Main 1989, 391–94.

Jürgen Habermas, 'Briefwechsel mit Kurt Sontheimer' ['Correspondence with Kurt Sontheimer'], in *Kleine Politische Schriften I–IV* ['Shorter political writings I–IV'], Frankfurt am Main 1981, 367–406.

Jürgen Habermas, 'Chemische Ferien vom Ich: Huxleys Umgang mit Meskalin' ['Chemical holidays from the ego: Huxley's use of mescaline'], in *Frankfurter Allgemeine Zeitung*, 11 December 1954.

Jürgen Habermas, 'Citizenship and National Identity', in *Between Facts and Norms: Contributions to a Discourse Theory of Law and Democracy*, trans. William Rehg, Cambridge, MA 1996, 491–515.

Jürgen Habermas, 'The Classical Doctrine of Politics in Relation to Social Philosophy', in *Theory and Practice*, trans. John Viertel, Boston, MA 1974, 41–81.

Jürgen Habermas, 'Core Europe as a Counterpower?' Follow-up Questions', in *The Divided West*, trans. Ciaran Cronin, Cambridge 2006, 49–56.

Jürgen Habermas, *The Crisis of the European Union: A Response*, trans. Ciaran Cronin, Cambridge 2012.

Jürgen Habermas, 'Deliberative Democracy: An Interview', in *A New Structural Transformation of the Public Sphere and Deliberative Politics*, trans. Ciaran Cronin, Cambridge 2023, 60–80.

Jürgen Habermas, 'The Dialectics of Rationalization' (interview with Axel Honneth, Eberhard Knödler-Bunte and Arno Widmann), trans. Leslie Adelson, Philip Boehm, Barton Byg, Karen Jankowski and Istvan Varkonyi, in Peter Dews (ed.), *Autonomy and Solidarity: Interviews with Jürgen Habermas*, New York 1992, 95–130.

Jürgen Habermas, 'Does Europe Need a Constitution?' in *Time of Transitions*, Cambridge 2006, 89–110.

Jürgen Habermas, 'Europe's Mistake' (interview), trans. Max Pensky, in *Granta*, 165 (23 November 2023), 177–85.

Jürgen Habermas, 'February 15, or: What Binds Europeans', in *The Divided West*, trans. Ciaran Cronin, Cambridge 2006, 39–48.

Jürgen Habermas, 'Fundamentalism and Terror', in *The Divided West*, trans. Ciaran Cronin, Cambridge 2006, 3–25.

Jürgen Habermas, 'The German Idealism of the Jewish Philosophers', in *Philosophical-Political Profiles*, trans. Frederick G. Lawrence, Cambridge, MA 1983, 21–44.

Jürgen Habermas, 'Gershom Scholem: The Torah in Disguise', in *Philosophical-Political Profiles*, trans. Frederick G. Lawrence, Cambridge, MA 1983, 199–211.

Jürgen Habermas, 'Heinrich Heine and the Role of the Intellectual in Germany', in *The New Conservatism: Cultural Criticism and the Historians' Debate*, trans. Shierry Weber Nicholsen, Cambridge, MA 1991, 71–99.

Jürgen Habermas, 'Historical Consciousness and Post-Traditional Identity: The Federal Republic's Orientation to the West', in *The New Conservatism: Cultural Criticism and the Historians' Debate*, trans. Shierry Weber Nicholsen, Cambridge, MA 1991, 249–68.

180     References

Jürgen Habermas, 'History and Evolution', trans. David J. Parent, in *Telos*, 39 (1979), 5–44.

Jürgen Habermas, 'The Horizon of Modernity is Shifting', in *Postmetaphysical Thinking: Philosophical Essays*, trans. William Mark Hohengarten, Cambridge, MA 1992, 3–9.

Jürgen Habermas, 'Ich bin alt, aber nicht fromm geworden' ['I have grown old, but not religious'], in Michael Funken (ed.), *Über Habermas: Gespräche mit Zeitgenossen*, 2nd edn., Darmstadt 2009, 197–206.

Jürgen Habermas, 'Ideologies and Society in the Post-war World' (interview with Gad Freudenthal), trans. Rodney Livingstone, in Peter Dews (ed.), *Autonomy and Solidarity: Interviews with Jürgen Habermas*, New York 1992, 43–62.

Jürgen Habermas, 'Interpreting the Fall of a Monument', trans. Max Pensky, in *German Law Journal*, 4, no. 7 (1 July 2003), 701–8.

Jürgen Habermas, 'An Interview with Jurgen Habermas' (interviewed by Mikael Carleheden and Rene Gabriels), in *Theory, Culture and Society* 13, no. 3 (1996), 1–18.

Jürgen Habermas, 'Ein Interview mit der *New Left Review*' ['An interview with the *New Left Review*'], in *Die Neue Unübersichtlichkeit: Kleine Politische Schriften V* ['The new obscurity: Shorter political writings V'], Frankfurt am Main 1985, 213–60.

Jürgen Habermas, 'An Interview on War and Peace', in *The Divided West*, trans. Ciaran Cronin, Cambridge 2006, 85–112.

Jürgen Habermas, 'Introduction', in Habermas (ed.), *Observations on 'The Spiritual Situation of the Age': Contemporary German Perspectives*, trans. Andrew Buchweiler, Cambridge, MA 1984, 1–30.

Jürgen Habermas, 'Is the Development of a European Identity Necessary, and Is It Possible?', in *The Divided West*, trans. Ciaran Cronin, Cambridge 2006, 67–82.

Jürgen Habermas, 'Karl Jaspers über Schelling' ['Karl Jaspers on Schelling'], in *Philosophisch-politische Profile*, Frankfurt am Main 1987, 82–7.

Jürgen Habermas, 'Keine Normalisierung der Vergangenheit' ['No normalization of the past'], in *Eine Art Schadensabwicklung, Kleine Politische Schriften VI* ['A kind of damage settlement: Shorter political writings VI'], Frankfurt am Main 1987, 11–17.

Jürgen Habermas, *Knowledge and Human Interests*, trans. Jeremy J. Shapiro, Boston, MA 1971.

Jürgen Habermas, 'Knowledge and Human Interests: A General Perspective', trans. Jeremy J. Shapiro, in *Knowledge and Human Interests*, Boston, MA 1971, 301–17.

Jürgen Habermas, 'Können komplexe Gesellschaften eine vernünftige Identität ausbilden?' ['Can complex societies form a rational identity?'], in *Zur Rekonstruktion des historischen Materialismus* ['On the reconstruction of historical materialism], Frankfurt am Main 1976, 92–128 [partially translated as 'On Social Identity', in *Telos*, 19 (1974), 91–103].

Jürgen Habermas, 'Labour and Interaction: Remarks on Hegel's Jena *Philosophy of Mind*', in *Theory and Practice*, trans. John Viertel, Boston, MA 1974, 142–69.

Jürgen Habermas, 'Im Lichte Heideggers' ['In the light of Heidegger'], in *Frankfurter Allgemeine Zeitung*, 12 July 1952.

Jürgen Habermas, 'Die Liebe zur Freiheit' ['The love of freedom'], in *Frankfurter Allgemeine Zeitung*, 18 June 2009.

Jürgen Habermas, '"Martin Heidegger? Nazi, sicher ein Nazi!" Ein Gespräch mit Jürgen Habermas' ['"Martin Heidegger? A Nazi, certainly a Nazi!" A conversation with Jürgen Habermas'], in Jürg Altwegg, ed., *Die Heidegger-Kontroverse* ['The Heidegger controversy'], Frankfurt am Main 1988, 172–75.

Jürgen Habermas, 'Martin Heidegger: On the Publication of Lectures from the Year 1935', in *Graduate Faculty Philosophy Journal*, 6, no. 2 (1977), 155–80.

Jürgen Habermas, 'Meine Jahre mit Helmut Kohl' ['My years with Helmut Kohl'], in *Die Zeit*, 11 March 1994.

Jürgen Habermas, 'Mit dem Pfeil ins Herz der Gegenwart: Zu Foucaults Vorlesung über Kants *Was ist Aufklärung*' ['With an arrow into the heart of the present: Foucault's lecture on Kant's

"What is Enlightenment"'], in *Die Neue Unübersichtlichkeit: Kleine Politische Schriften V* ['The new obscurity: Shorter political writings V'], Frankfurt am Main 1985, 126–31.

Jürgen Habermas, 'Modernity: An Incomplete Project', trans. Seyla Ben-Habib, in Hal Foster (ed.), *The Anti-Aesthetic: Essays on Postmodern Culture*, Seattle 1983, 3–15.

Jürgen Habermas, 'Moral Universalism at a Time of Political Regression: A Conversation with Jürgen Habermas about the Present and His Life's Work', interview with Claudia Czingon, Aletta Diefenbach and Victor Kempf, in *Theory, Culture and Society*, 37, nos. 7–8 (2020), 11–36.

Jürgen Habermas, *Die nachholende Revolution: Kleine Politische Schriften VII* ['The rectifying revolution: Shorter political writings VII'], Frankfurt am Main 1990.

Jürgen Habermas, 'The New Intimacy between Culture and Politics: Theses on Enlightenment in Germany', in *The New Conservatism: Cultural Criticism and the Historians' Debate*, trans. Shierry Weber Nicholsen, Cambridge, MA 1991, 197–206.

Jurgen Habermas, 'The New Obscurity: The Crisis of the Welfare State and the Exhaustion of Utopian Energies', in *The New Conservatism: Cultural Criticism and the Historians' Debate*, trans. Shierry Weber Nicholsen, Cambridge, MA 1991, 48–70.

Jürgen Habermas, *A New Structural Transformation of the Public Sphere and Deliberative Politics*, trans. Ciaran Cronin, Cambridge 2023.

Jürgen Habermas, *The Past as Future*, trans. Max Pensky, Lincoln, NE 1994.

Jürgen Habermas, *The Philosophical Discourse of Modernity: Twelve Lectures*, trans. Frederick Lawrence, Cambridge, MA 1990.

Jürgen Habermas, 'A Philosophico-Political Profile' (interview with Perry Anderson and Peter Dews), trans. Peter Dews, in Peter Dews (ed.), *Autonomy and Solidarity: Interviews with Jürgen Habermas*, New York 1992, 147–86. (First published in *New Left Review*, no. 151 (May–June 1985), 75–105.)

Jürgen Habermas, 'Philosophie ist Risiko' ['Philosophy is risk-taking'], in *Frankfurter Allgemeine Zeitung*, 19 June 1954.

Jürgen Habermas, 'Philosophy and Science as Literature?', in *Postmetaphysical Thinking: Philosophical Essays*, trans. William Mark Hohengarten, Cambridge, MA 1992, 205–27.

Jürgen Habermas, 'Philosophy as Stand-In and Interpreter', in *Moral Consciousness and Communicative Action*, trans. Christian Lenhardt and Shierry Weber Nicholsen, Cambridge, MA 1990, 1–20.

Jürgen Habermas, 'A Plea for Negotiations', trans. Ciaran Cronin, in *SZ.de*, 14 February 2023, https://www.sueddeutsche.de/pro jekte/artikel/kultur/juergen-habermas-ukraine-sz-negotiations-e480179/. [Original German publication: 'Krieg und Empörung', in *Süddeutsche Zeitung*, 28 April 2022.]

Jürgen Habermas, 'Political Culture in Germany since 1968: An Interview with Dr. Rainer Erd for the *Frankfurter Rundschau*' [11 March 1988], in *The New Conservatism: Cultural Criticism and the Historians' Debate*, trans. Shierry Weber Nicholsen, Cambridge, MA 1991, 183–95.

Jürgen Habermas, 'Political Experience and the Renewal of Marxist Theory' (interview with Detlef Horster and Willem van Reijen), trans. Ron Smith, in Peter Dews (ed.), *Autonomy and Solidarity: Interviews with Jürgen Habermas*, New York 1992, 77–94.

Jürgen Habermas, 'Psychischer Thermidor und die Wiedergeburt einer rebellischen Subjektivität' ['The psychological thermidor and the rebirth of a rebellious subjectivity'], in *Philosophisch-politische Profile*, Frankfurt am Main 1987, 319–35.

Jürgen Habermas, 'Public Space and Political Public Sphere: The Biographical Roots of Two Motifs in My Thought', in *Between Naturalism and Religion: Philosophical Essays*, trans. Ciaran Cronin, Cambridge 2008, 11–23.

Jürgen Habermas, 'On the Public Use of History: The Official Self-Understanding of the Federal Republic is Breaking Up', in *Forever in the Shadow of Hitler? Original Documents of the* Historikerstreit, *the Controversy Concerning the Singularity of the Holocaust*, trans.

James Knowlton and Truett Cates, Atlantic Heights, NJ 1993, 162–70.

Jürgen Habermas, 'Die Scheinrevolution und ihre Kinder' ['The illusory revolution and its children'], in *Kleine Politische Schriften I–IV* ['Shorter political writings I–IV'], Frankfurt am Main 1981, 249–60.

Jürgen Habermas, 'Schlusswort' ['Conclusion'], in *50 Jahre Grundgesetz – 35 Jahre Theodor-Heuss-Stiftung: Auf dem Wege zu einer demokratischen Bürgergesellschaft* ['The constitution at 50; the Theodor Heuss Foundation at 35: On the way to a democratic society of citizens'], Stuttgart 1999, 36–40.

Jürgen Habermas, 'Some Conditions for Revolutionizing Late Capitalist Societies', in *Canadian Journal of Political and Social Theory*, 7, nos. 1–2 (1983), 35–45.

Jürgen Habermas, 'Statt eines Vorworts' ['In lieu of a foreword'], in Saul Friedländer et al. (eds.), *Verbrechen ohne Namen: Anmerkungen zum neuen Streit über den Holocaust*, Munich 2022, 8–13.

Jürgen Habermas, *Structural Transformation of the Public Sphere: An Inquiry into a Category of Bourgeois Society*, trans. Thomas Burger, with Frederick Lawrence, Cambridge, MA 1991.

Jürgen Habermas, 'Die Stunde der nationalen Empfindung: Republikanische Gesinnung oder Nationalbewußtsein?' ['The hour of national feeling: Republican convictions or national consciousness?'], in *Die nachholende Revolution: Kleine Politische Schriften VII*, Frankfurt am Main 1990, 157–66.

Jürgen Habermas, 'Taking Aim at the Heart of the Present: On Foucault's Lecture on Kant's *What Is Enlightenment?*', in *The New Conservatism: Cultural Criticism and the Historians' Debate*, trans. Shierry Weber Nicholsen, Cambridge, MA 1991, 173–80.

Jürgen Habermas, 'A Test for Popular Justice: The Accusations against the Intellectuals', trans. Mark Franke, in *New German Critique*, 12 (Fall 1977), 11–13.

Jürgen Habermas, *The Theory of Communicative Action*, vol. 1, *Reason and the Rationalization of Society*, trans. Thomas McCarthy, Cambridge 1984.

Jürgen Habermas, *The Theory of Communicative Action*, vol. 2, *Lifeworld and System: A Critique of Functionalist Reason*, trans. Thomas McCarthy, Cambridge 1987.

Jürgen Habermas, 'Truth and Society: The Discursive Redemption of Factual Claims to Validity', in *On the Pragmatics of Social Interaction: Preliminary Studies in the Theory of Communicative Action*, trans. Barbara Fultner, Cambridge, MA 2001.

Jürgen Habermas, 'Über den moralischen Notstand in der Bundesrepublik' ['On the moral emergency in the Federal Republic of Germany'], in *Philosophisch-politische Profile*, Frankfurt am Main 1987, 96–100.

Jürgen Habermas, 'Über Titel, Texte und Termine oder wie man den Zeitgeist reflektiert' ['On titles, texts and dates, or how to reflect the *zeitgeist*'], in *Die nachholende Revolution: Kleine Politische Schriften VII*, Frankfurt am Main 1990, 48–50.

Jürgen Habermas, 'Vier Jungkonservative beim Projektleiter der Moderne' ['Four young conservatives with the project manager of modernity'], in *die tageszeitung*, 3 and 21 October 1980.

Jürgen Habermas, 'Vorbereitende Bemerkungen zu einer Theorie der kommunikativen Kompetenz' ['Preliminary remarks on a theory of communicative competence'], in Jürgen Habermas and Niklas Luhmann, *Theorie der Gesellschaft oder Sozialtechnologie: Was leistet die Systemforschung?* Frankfurt am Main 1971, 101–41.

Jürgen Habermas, 'Vorwort' ['Preface'], in *Die Neue Unübersichtlichkeit: Kleine Politische Schriften V* ['The new obscurity: Shorter political writings V'], Frankfurt am Main 1985, 7–9.

Jürgen Habermas, 'Vorwort' ['Preface'], in *Politik, Kunst, Religion: Essays über zeitgenössische Philosophen* ['Politics, art religion: Essays on contemporary philosophers'], Stuttgart, 1978, 3–10.

Jürgen Habermas, 'Vorwort zur Neuauflage 1990' ['Preface to the new 1990 edition'], in *Strukturwandel der Öffentlichkeit: Untersuchungen zu einer Kategorie der bürgerlichen Gesellschaft*, Frankfurt am Main 1996, 11–50.

Jürgen Habermas, 'War and Indignation: The West's Red Line Dilemma', in *SZ.de*, 28 April 2022, https://www.sueddeutsche.de

/projekte/artikel/kultur/the-dilemma-of-the-west-juergen-haber
mas-on-the-war-in-ukraine-e032431/.

Jürgen Habermas, 'What Does Socialism Mean Today? The Rectifying
Revolution and the Need for New Thinking on the Left', in *New
Left Review*, no. 183 (1990), 3–21.

Jürgen Habermas, 'Why More Philosophy?', trans. E. B. Ashton, in
*Social Research*, 38, no. 4 (1971), 633–54.

Jürgen Habermas, 'Wider die Logik des Krieges: Ein Plädoyer für
Zurückhaltung, aber nicht gegenüber Israel' ['Against the logic
of war: A plea for reserve, but not towards Israel'], in *Die Zeit*,
15 February 1991.

Jürgen Habermas, 'Yet Again: German Identity; A Unified Nation of
Angry DM-Burghers?', in *New German Critique*, no. 52 (1991),
84–101.

Jürgen Habermas, 'Ziviler Ungehorsam – Testfall für den demokratischen Rechtsstaat' ['Civil disobedience: Test case for
constitutional democracy'], in *Die Neue Unübersichtlichkeit:
Kleine Politische Schriften V* ['The new obscurity: Shorter political
writings V'], Frankfurt am Main 1985, 79–99.

Jürgen Habermas et al., 'Grundsätze der Solidarität: Eine
Stellungnahme' ['Principles of solidarity: A statement'], 2023,
https://www.normativeorders.net/2023/grundsatze-der-solidari
tat/.

'Habermas plädiert für schnelle Verhandlungen' ['Habermas advocates rapid negotiations'], *Süddeutsche Zeitung*, 15 February
2023.

'Habermas als Popstar' ['Habermas as a pop star'], in *Frankfurter
Allgemeine Zeitung*, 14 October 2001.

Lutz Hachmeister, *Heideggers Testament: Der Philosoph, der Spiegel
und die SS* ['Heidegger's last will: The philosopher, *Der Spiegel* and
the SS], Berlin 2015.

Jens Hacke, 'Wir-Gefühle: Repräsentationsformen kollektiver
Identität bei Jürgen Habermas' ['Feelings of "we": Forms of repre-
sentation of collective identity in Jürgen Habermas'], in *Mittelweg
36*, no. 6 (2008), 12–32.

François Hartog, *Régimes d'historicité: Présentisme et expériences du temps* [Regimes of historicity: Presentism and experiences of time], Paris 2003.

Winfried Heidemann, 'Die Verfolgung und Ermordung der Theorie durch die Praxis, dargestellt von Jürgen Habermas' ['The persecution and murder of theory by practice, as represented by Jürgen Habermas'], in *Frankfurter Schule und Studentenbewegung: Von der Flaschenpost zum Molotowcocktail, 1946–1995* ['The Frankfurt School and the student movement: From message in a bottle to Molotov cocktail'], vol. 2: *Dokumente*, Hamburg 1998, 733–5.

Dieter Henrich, *Ins Denken ziehen: Eine philosophische Autobiographie* ['Moving into thought: a philosophical autobiography'], Munich 2021.

Dieter Henrich, 'What Is Metaphysics? What Is Modernity? Twelve Theses against Jürgen Habermas', in Peter Dews (ed.), *Habermas: A Critical Reader*, Oxford 1999, 291–319.

Ulrich Herbert, 'Der Historikerstreit: Politische, wissenschaftliche, biographische Aspekte' ['The historians' dispute: Political, academic and biographical aspects'], in Martin Sabrow et al. (eds.), *Zeitgeschichte als Streitgeschichte: Große Kontroversen nach 1945* ['Contemporary history as a history of disputes: Major controversies since 1945'], Munich 2003, 94–113.

Ulrich Herbert, *A History of Twentieth-Century Germany*, trans. Ben Fowkes, New York 2019.

Raul Hilberg, *Die Vernichtung der europäischen Juden* [*The Destruction of the European Jews*], new expanded edn., Frankfurt am Main 2023.

Klaus Hildebrand, 'Das Zeitalter der Tyrannen: Eine Entgegnung auf Jürgen Habermas', in *'Historikerstreit': Die Dokumentation der Kontroverse um die Einzigartigkeit der nationalsozialistischen Judenvernichtung*, Munich 1988, 84–92.

Axel Honneth, 'Adorno und Habermas: Zur kommunikationstheoretischen Wende kritischer Sozialphilosophie' ['Adorno and Habermas: On critical social philosophy's turn to communication theory'], in *Merkur*, 374 (1979), 648–65.

Michael G. Horowitz, 'Portrait of the Marxist as an Old Trouper', in *Playboy*, September 1970.

Peter Iden, 'Alles Linke auf seine Kappe: Ein Gespräch mit Jürgen Habermas – aus Anlaß seiner Auszeichnung mit dem Adorno-Preis' ['Responsibility for the whole Left: A conversation with Jürgen Habermas on the occasion of his receiving the Adorno Prize'], in *Frankfurter Rundschau*, 11 September 1980.

Florian Illies, 'Jahrgang 1929' ['The 1929 cohort'], in *Die Zeit*, 12 March 2009.

Urs Jaeggi, 'Versöhnung als Puzzlearbeit: Nachdenken über die "Theorie des kommunikativen Handelns" von Jürgen Habermas' ['Reconciliation as working a puzzle: Reflections on *The Theory of Communicative Action* by Jürgen Habermas'], in *Die Zeit*, 2 April 1982.

Lorenz Jäger, *Walter Benjamin: Das Leben eines Unvollendeten* [Walter Benjamin: The life of an unfinished man], Berlin 2017.

Ulrike Jureit and Christian Schneider, *Gefühlte Opfer: Illusionen der Vergangenheitsbewältigung* ['Sensed victims: Illusions of coming to terms with the past'], Stuttgart 2010.

Jürgen Kaube, 'Die geistige Situation der Zeit: Über einige Merkmale von Gegenwartsdiagnosen' ['The spiritual situation of the age: On some characteristics of diagnoses of the present'], in Reinhard Schulz et al. (eds.), *'Wahrheit ist, was uns verbindet': Karl Jaspers' Kunst zu philosophieren* ['"Truth is what connects us": Karl Jaspers's art of philosophizing'], Göttingen 2008, 379–90.

Jürgen Kaube, 'Geschichtspatriotismus: Über einige Ähnlichkeiten der Gegner im Historikerstreit' ['Historical patriotism: On some similarities between the opponents in the Historians' Dispute'], in Mathias Brodkorb (ed.), *Singuläres Auschwitz? Ernst Nolte, Jürgen Habermas und 25 Jahre 'Historikerstreit'* ['Singular Auschwitz? Ernst Nolte, Jürgen Habermas and 25 years since the "Historikerstreit"'], Banzkow 2011, 115–20.

Jozef Keulartz, *De verkeerde wereld van Jürgen Habermas* ['The upside-down world of Jürgen Habermas'], Amsterdam 1992.

Alexander Kluge, '"Unheimlichkeit der Zeit": Neue Geschichten, Hefte 1–18' ['The uncanniness of time: New stories, books 1–18'], in *Chronik der Gefühle*, vol. 2: *Lebensläufe*, Frankfurt am Main 2000, 9–453.

Andreas Koch, 'Einfamilienhaussoziologie' ['Single-family house sociology'], https://www.waahr.de/texte/einfamilienhaussoziologie.

*Kollektive Erinnerungsprozesse in Beziehung zur NS-Zeit* ['Collective processes of remembering in relation to the Nazi period'], unpublished colloquium transcript, 14–15 February 1986, in the library of the Institute for Advanced Study (*Wissenschaftskolleg*), Berlin.

Andreas Koller, 'Counterfactual Presuppositions', in Hauke Brunkhorst et al. (eds.), *Habermas Handbook*, New York 2017, 520–7.

Reinhart Koselleck,' Wozu noch Historie?' ['Why more history?'], in *Historische Zeitschrift*, 212 (1971), 1–18.

Ivan Krastev and Stephen Holmes, *The Light that Failed: A Reckoning*, London 2019.

Joachim Krause, 'Eskalationsphobie – eine deutsche Krankheit' ['Escalation phobia: A German disorder'], in *Frankfurter Allgemeine Zeitung*, 7 February 2023.

Jörg Lau, 'Öffentlichkeit und Beharrung: 65 und immer noch im Ring: Jürgen Habermas, Kommunikationsphilosoph und Historikerstreiter, hat morgen Geburtstag' ['Public sphere and persistence: 65 and still in the ring; tomorrow is the birthday of Jürgen Habermas, philosopher of communication and disputer of historians'], in *taz*, 17 June 1994.

Ariane Leendertz, 'Ungunst des Augenblicks: Das "MPI zur Erforschung der Lebensbedingungen der technisch-industriellen Welt" in Starnberg' ['The inauspicious moment: The Max Planck Institute for the Study of the Scientific-Technical World in Starnberg'], in *Indes: Zeitschrift für Politik und Gesellschaft*, 3, no. 1 (2014) 105–16.

Per Leo, *Tränen ohne Trauer: Nach der Erinnerungskultur*, Stuttgart 2021.

Hermann Lübbe, 'Der Nationalsozialismus im deutschen Nachkriegsbewusstsein' ['Nazism in the German postwar consciousness'], in *Historische Zeitschrift*, 236 (1983), 579–99.

Niklas Luhmann, *Social Systems*, trans. John Bednarz, Jr., with Dirk Baecker, Palo Alto, 1995.

Niklas Luhmann, 'Systemtheoretische Argumentationen' ['Arguments of systems theory'], in Habermas and Luhmann, *Theorie der Gesellschaft oder Sozialtechnologie: Was leistet die Systemforschung?* ['Theory of society or social technology: What does systems research achieve?'], Frankfurt am Main 1971, 291–405.

Niklas Maak, 'Die absolute Form und die Geschichte: Betrachtungen zum Haus Habermas' ['Absolute form and history: Observations on the Habermas house'], in *Zeitschrift für Ideengeschichte*, 15, no. 3 (2021), 101–14.

Charles S. Maier, *The Unmasterable Past: History, Holocaust, and German National Identity*, Cambridge, MA 1988.

Golo Mann, 'The Old History and the New: Thoughts on the Crisis of Theory and Practice', in *Encounter*, 51, no. 2 (1978), 11–17.

Karl Markus Michel, 'Der Grundwortschatz des wissenschaftlichen Gesamtarbeiters seit der szientifischen Wende' ['The basic vocabulary of the academic all-round worker since the scientific turn'], in *Stichworte zur 'Geistigen Situation der Zeit'* ['Keywords on the "spiritual situation of the time"'], vol. 2: *Politik und Kultur*, ed. Jürgen Habermas, Frankfurt am Main 1979, 817–41.

Karl Markus Michel, review of Jürgen Habermas's *Theorie des kommunikativen Handelns*, in *Der Spiegel*, 12 (March 1982).

Odo Marquard, *Schwierigkeiten mit der Geschichtsphilosophie* ['Difficulties with the philosophy of history'], Frankfurt am Main 1973.

James Miller, *The Passion of Michel Foucault*, New York 1993.

Christoph Möllers, 'Ach, Ästhetik!' ['Oh, aesthetics!'], in *Zeitschrift für Ideengeschichte*, 15, no. 3 (2021), 81–5.

Wolfgang Mommsen, *Die Geschichtswissenschaft jenseits des Historismus* ['The study of history beyond historicism'], Düsseldorf 1971.

A. Dirk Moses, 'Deutschlands Erinnerungskultur und der "Terror der Geschichte"' ['Germany's commemorative culture and the "terror of history"'], in Susan Neiman and Michael Wildt (eds.), *Historiker streiten: Gewalt und Holocaust; Die Debatte*, Berlin 2022, 199–242.

A. Dirk Moses, *German Intellectuals and the Nazi Past*, Cambridge 2007.

A. Dirk Moses, 'Der Katechismus der Deutschen' ['The Germans' catechism'], https://geschichtedergegenwart.ch/der-katechismus -der-deutschen.

Stefan Müller-Doohm, *Habermas: A Biography*, trans. Daniel Steuer, Cambridge 2016.

Susan Neiman, 'Wie die beiden Historikerstreite zusammen-hängen' ['How the two historians' disputes are connected'], in Susan Neiman and Michael Wildt (eds.), *Historiker streiten: Gewalt und Holocaust; Die Debatte* ['Historians argue. Violence and the Holocaust: The debate'], Berlin 2022, 7–18.

Susan Neiman and Michael Wildt (eds.), *Historiker streiten: Gewalt und Holocaust; Die Debatte* ['Historians argue. Violence and the Holocaust: The debate'], Berlin 2022.

Peter Neumann, 'Seine Sorge: Warum Jürgen Habermas noch immer in den Kategorien der Welt vor 1989 denkt' ['His concern: Why Jürgen Habermas is still thinking in the categories of the pre-1989 world'], in *Die Zeit*, 23 February 2023.

Thomas Nipperdey, 'Unter der Herrschaft des Verdachts: Wissenschaftliche Aussagen dürfen nicht an ihrer politischen Funktion gemessen werden' ['Dominated by suspicion: Scientific statements must not be judged by their political function'], in *'Historikerstreit': Die Dokumentation der Kontroverse um die Einzigartigkeit der nationalsozialistischen Judenvernichtung* ['"Historians' dispute": Documenting the controversy surrounding the uniqueness of the National Socialist extermination of the Jews'], Munich 1988, 215–19.

Thomas Nipperdey, 'Wozu Geschichte gut ist' ['What history is good for'], in *Militärgeschichtliche Zeitschrift*, 41, no. 1 (1987), 7–13.

Ernst Nolte, 'Vergangenheit, die nicht vergehen will' ['A past that does not want to pass away'], in *Frankfurter Allgemeine Zeitung*, 6 June 1986.

Hanns-Josef Ortheil, '"Königsweg der Individuation": Philosophie; Literatur; Bildung' ['Royal road of individuation: Philosophy, literature, education'], in Michael Rutschky (ed.), *Errungenschaften: Eine Kasuistik* ['Achievements: A case history'], Frankfurt am Main 1982, 203–43.

Morten Paul, *Suhrkamp Theorie: Eine Buchreihe im philosophischen Nachkrieg* ['Suhrkamp *Theorie*: A book series in the philosophical postwar period'], Leipzig 2022.

Max Pensky, 'Jürgen Habermas and the Antinomies of the Intellectual', in Peter Dews (ed.), *Habermas: A Critical Reader*, Oxford 1999, 211–37.

Max Pensky, 'Universalism and the Situated Critic', in Stephen K. White (ed.), *The Cambridge Companion to Habermas*, Cambridge 1995, 67–94.

Klaus Pokatzky, 'Saul Friedländer: Pavel, Paul, Shaul: Erfahrungen mit der deutschen Verdrängung; Ein Historiker aus Tel Aviv in Berlin' ['Pavel, Paul, Shaul: Experiences with German repression; A historian from Tel Aviv in Berlin'], in *Die Zeit*, 16 May 1986.

Till van Rahden, 'Die Gummersbacher Schule: Hans-Ulrich Wehler inszeniert eine Debatte' ['The Gummersbach School: Hans-Ulrich Wehler stages a debate'], in *Zeitschrift für Ideengeschichte*, 15, no. 3 (2021), 6–10.

Hans-Christoph Rauh, *Philosophie aus einer abgeschlossenen Welt: Zur Geschichte der DDR-Philosophie und ihrer Institutionen* ['Philosophy from an isolated world: On the history of East German philosophy and its institutions'], Berlin 2017.

Ulrich Raulff, 'Akute Zeichen fiebriger Dekonstruktion: Die Frankfurter Schule und ihre Gegenspieler in Paris: Eine Verkennungsgeschichte aus gegebenem Anlass' ['Acute symptoms of feverish deconstruction: The Frankfurt School and its antagonists in Paris; A story of misjudgement in light of recent events'], in *Süddeutsche Zeitung*, 21 September 2001.

Jan Philipp Reemtsma, 'Erinnerung vergemeinschaften: Ein kurzes Gespräch über Nachteile der Geschichtsschreibung' ['Communalizing memory: A brief conversation about drawbacks of history writing'], in *Mittelweg 36*, no. 3 (2006), 29–36.

Jan Philipp Reemtsma, 'Auf den Friedenspreisträger 2001: Eine Laudatio' ['In praise of the 2001 Peace Prize laureate'], https://www.friedenspreis-des-deutschen-buchhandels.de/alle-preistrae ger-seit-1950/2000-2009/juergen-habermas.

Andreas Rödder, *21.0: Eine kurze Geschichte der Gegenwart* ['21.0: A brief history of the present'], Berlin 2015.

Jan Ross, 'Hegel der Bundesrepublik' ['The Hegel of West Germany'], in *Die Zeit*, 11 October 2001.

Moritz Rudolph, 'Tocqueville global: Das Phantom des schrecklichen Westens' ['Global Tocqueville: The spectre of the terrible West'], in *Merkur*, 893 (2023), 84–91.

Michael Rutschky, *Gegen Ende: Tagebuchaufzeichnungen 1996– 2009* ['Towards the end: Journal notes, 1996–2009'], Berlin 2019.

Michael Rutschky, *Mitgeschrieben: Die Sensation des Gewöhnlichen* ['Noted: The sensation of the ordinary'], Berlin 2015.

Michael Rutschky, *Wartezeit: Ein Sittenbild* ['Waiting: A genre scene'], Cologne 1983.

Michael Rutschky, 'Der Zwischenraum: Stücke zu einer Theorie des Soziotops' ['The interstice: Fragments of a theory of the socio-tope'], in *Errungenschaften: Eine Kasuistik* ['Achievements: A case study'], Frankfurt am Main 1982, 378–406.

Philipp Sarasin, *1977: Eine kurze Geschichte der Gegenwart* ['A brief history of the present'], Frankfurt am Main 2021.

Marie-Luise Scherer, *Ungeheurer Alltag: Geschichten und Reportagen* ['Uncanny everyday life: Stories and reports'], Reinbek 1990.

Axel Schildt, *Medien-Intellektuelle in der Bundesrepublik* ['Media intellectuals in West Germany'], Göttingen 2020.

Christoph Schmidt, *Israel und die Geister von '68: Eine Phänomenologie* ['Israel and the ghosts of '68: A phenomenology'], Göttingen 2018.

Gershom Scholem, 'Address', in *Proceedings of the Fifth Plenary Assembly of the World Jewish Congress*, Brussels 1966, 219.

Gershom Scholem, 'Juden und Deutsche' ['Jews and Germans'], in *Judaica* II, Frankfurt am Main 1970, 47–54.

Danilo Scholz, 'Innerdeutsches Frankreich' ['Intra-German France'], in *Zeitschrift für Ideengeschichte*, 15, no. 3 (2021), 66–9.

Olaf Scholz, 'Ab und an lese ich auch Comics' ['From time to time I also read comics'], interview, in *Süddeutsche Zeitung*, 28 July 2023.

Elke Seefried, *Shaping Tomorrow's World: A Twentieth-Century History of West German, Cold War and Global Futures Studies*, New York 2024.

Gustav Seibt, 'Die Formen der Historie' ['The forms of history'], review of Pietro Rossi (ed.), *Theorie der modernen Geschichtsschreibung*, in *Merkur*, 463/64 (1987), 903–7.

Gustav Seibt, 'Zyklus von Erniedrigung und Überhebung: Norbert Elias' "Studien über die Deutschen"' ['Cycle of humiliation and arrogance: Norbert Elias's *Studies on the Germans*'], *Merkur*, 494 (1990), 330–4.

Quentin Skinner, 'Habermas's Reformation', in *New York Review of Books*, 7 October 1982, 35–8.

Timothy Snyder, 'Jürgen Habermas and Ukraine: Germans have been involved in the war, chiefly on the wrong side', in *FAZ.net*, 27 June 2022, https://www.faz.net/aktuell/politik/ausland/juergen-habermas-and-ukraine-germans-have-been-involved-in-the-war-18131718.html.

Robert Spaemann, 'Die Utopie der Herrschaftsfreiheit' ['The utopia of freedom from dominance'], in *Merkur*, 292 (1972), 735–52.

Jörg Später, 'Der Verlorene: George Lichtheim findet ein offenes Ohr' ['The lost man: George Lichtheim finds an open ear'], in *Zeitschrift für Ideengeschichte*, 15, no. 3 (2021), 34–8.

Matthew Specter, *Habermas: An Intellectual Biography*, Cambridge 2011.

Guido Sprügel, 'Der Katechet des Unsinns' ['The catechist of nonsense'], in *Jungle World*, 10 February 2022.

Botho Strauss, *Couples, Passersby*, trans. Roslyn Theobald, Evanston, IL 1996.

Simon Strauss, 'Hart verteidigte Illusionen: Der Chef-Kritiker der bundesrepublikanischen Öffentlichkeit sieht seine Felle davonschwimmen' ['Staunchly defended illusions: The head critic of the West German public sphere sees his hopes fading'], in *Frankfurter Allgemeine Zeitung*, 30 April 2022.

Christoph Türcke, 'Darüber schweigen sie alle: Tabu und Antinomie in der neuen Debatte über das Dritte Reich' ['All of them are silent about it: Taboo and antinomy in the new debate on the Third Reich'], in *Merkur*, 463/64 (1987), 762–72.

Siegfried Unseld, *Chronik 1970*, Frankfurt am Main 2010.

Nina Verheyen, *Diskussionslust: Eine Kulturgeschichte des 'besseren Arguments' in Westdeutschland* ['The joy of discussion: A cultural history of the "better argument" in West Germany'], Göttingen 2010.

'Verschwiegene Enteignung: Wer erfand die Wendung von der "Gnade der späten Geburt"?' ['Tacit appropriation: Who invented the expression "the mercy of a later birth"?'], in *Der Spiegel*, 14 September 1986.

Martin Walser, 'Experiences While Composing a Sunday Speech: The Peace Prize Speech', in Thomas A. Kovach and Martin Walser, *The Burden of the Past: Martin Walser on Modern German Identity; Texts, Contexts, Commentary*, Rochester, NY 2008.

Martin Walser, 'Handshake with Ghosts', in Thomas A. Kovach and Martin Walser, *The Burden of the Past. Martin Walser on Modern German Identity: Texts, Contexts, Commentary*, Rochester, NY 2008.

Martin Walser, *Leben und Schreiben: Tagebücher 1974–1978* ['Living and writing: Diaries, 1974–1978'], Reinbek 2012.

Martin Walser, *Schreiben und Leben: Tagebücher 1979–1981* ['Writing and living: Diaries, 1979–1981'], Reinbek 2015.

Andy Warhol and Pat Hackett, *POPism: The Warhol Sixties*, New York 1980.

Richard von Weizsäcker, 'Speech during the Ceremony Commemorating the 40th Anniversary of the End of War in Europe and of National-Socialist Tyranny on 8 May 1985 at the

Bundestag, Bonn', www.bundespraesident.de/SharedDocs/Down
loads/DE/Reden/2015/02/150202-RvW-Rede-8-Mai-1985-englisch.
pdf.

Arno Widmann, 'Wahrheit und Gesellschaft' ['Truth and society'], in
*Frankfurter Rundschau*, 26 January 2019.

Rolf Wiggershaus, *Jürgen Habermas*, Reinbek 2004.

Michael Wildt, review of Saul Friedländer et al., *Verbrechen ohne
Namen: Anmerkungen zum neuen Streit über den Holocaust*
['Crimes without names: Notes on the new debate about the
Holocaust'], Munich 2022, in *HSoz-Kult*, 13 May 2022.

Susann Witt-Stahl, 'Linksfaschismus: Erich Fried versucht einen
Bundesgenossen gegen sich selbst zu gewinnen' ['Left fascism:
Erich Fried tries to win an ally against himself'], in *Zeitschrift für
Ideengeschichte*, 15, no. 3 (2021), 43–5.

Christa Wolf, *Parting from Phantoms: Selected Writings, 1990–1994*,
trans. Jan van Heurck, Chicago 1997.

Tom Wolfe, 'Radical Chic: That Party at Lenny's', in *New York
Magazine*, 8 June 1970, 26–55.

Roman Yos, *Der junge Habermas: Eine ideengeschichtliche
Untersuchung seines Denkens 1952–1962* ['Young Habermas:
A study of his thought in relation to the history of philosophy,
1952–1962'], Frankfurt am Main 2019.

Lea Ypi, *Free: Coming of Age at the End of History*, London 2022.

# Index

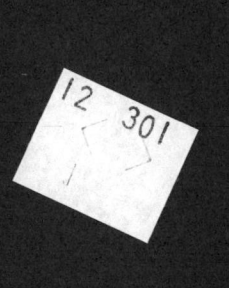